The Fundamental Princip
Financial Regulation

Geneva Reports on the World Economy 11

International Center for Monetary and Banking Studies (ICMB)

International Center for Monetary and Banking Studies
11 A Avenue de la Paix
1202 Geneva
Switzerland

Tel (41 22) 734 9548
Fax (41 22) 733 3853
Website: www.icmb.ch

Centre for Economic Policy Research (CEPR)

Centre for Economic Policy Research
53-56 Great Sutton Street
London EC1V 0DG
UK

Tel: +44 (0)20 7183 8801
Fax: +44 (0)20 7183 8820
Email: cepr@cepr.org
Website: www.cepr.org

British Library Cataloguing in Publication Data
A catalogue record for this book is available from the British Library

ISBN: 978-0-9557009-7-2

The Fundamental Principles of Financial Regulation

Geneva Reports on the World Economy 11

Markus Brunnermeier
Princeton University and CEPR

Andrew Crockett
JPMorgan Chase

Charles Goodhart
London School of Economics

Avinash D. Persaud
Intelligence Capital Limited

Hyun Song Shin
Princeton University and CEPR

Each author has contributed on a personal basis, and no responsibility should be attached to any institution to which that author either is or has been attached.

ICMB INTERNATIONAL CENTER
FOR MONETARY
AND BANKING STUDIES

CIMB CENTRE INTERNATIONAL
D'ETUDES MONETAIRES
ET BANCAIRES

International Center for Monetary and Banking Studies (ICMB)

The International Center for Monetary and Banking Studies was created in 1973 as an independent, non-profit foundation. It is associated with Geneva's Graduate Institute of International Studies. Its aim is to foster exchange of views between the financial sector, central banks and academics on issues of common interest. It is financed through grants from banks, financial institutions and central banks.

The Center sponsors international conferences, public lectures, original research and publications. It has earned a solid reputation in the Swiss and international banking community where it is known for its contribution to bridging the gap between theory and practice in the field of international banking and finance.

In association with CEPR, the Center launched a new series of *Geneva Reports on the World Economy* in 1999. The eight subsequent volumes have attracted considerable interest among practitioners, policy-makers and scholars working on the reform of international financial architecture.

The ICMB is non-partisan and does not take any view on policy. Its publications, including the present report, reflect the opinions of the authors, not of ICMB or of any of its sponsoring institutions.

Centre for Economic Policy Research (CEPR)

The Centre for Economic Policy Research is a network of over 700 Research Fellows and Affiliates, based primarily in European universities. The Centre coordinates the research activities of its Fellows and Affiliates and communicates the results to the public and private sectors. CEPR is an entrepreneur, developing research initiatives with the producers, consumers and sponsors of research. Established in 1983, CEPR is a European economics research organization with uniquely wide-ranging scope and activities.

The Centre is pluralist and non-partisan, bringing economic research to bear on the analysis of medium- and long-run policy questions. CEPR research may include views on policy, but the Executive Committee of the Centre does not give prior review to its publications, and the Centre takes no institutional policy positions. The opinions expressed in this report are those of the authors and not those of the Centre for Economic Policy Research.

About the Authors

Markus K. Brunnermeier is the Edwards S. Sanford Professor at Princeton University. He is a faculty member of the Department of Economics and affiliated with Princeton's Bendheim Center for Finance and the International Economics Section. He is also a research associate at CEPR, NBER and CESifo, and an academic consultant to the Federal Reserve Bank of New York. He was awarded his Ph.D. by the London School of Economics (LSE), where he was also affiliated with its Financial Markets Group. He is a Sloan Research Fellow, and recipient of the German Bernácer Prize granted for outstanding contributions in the fields of macroeconomics and finance.

He is primarily interested in studying financial crises, bubbles and significant mispricings due to institutional frictions, strategic considerations, and behavioral trading. His research also explains why liquidity dries up when it is needed most and has important implications for risk management and financial regulation. He is also an associate editor of the *American Economic Review, Journal of European Economic Association, Journal of Finance, Journal of Financial Intermediation* and was previously on the editorial board of the *Review of Financial Studies*.

Charles Goodhart, CBE, FBA is a member of the Financial Markets Group at the London School of Economics, having previously, 1987-2005, been its Deputy Director. Until his retirement in 2002, he had been the Norman Sosnow Professor of Banking and Finance at LSE since 1985. Before then, he had worked at the Bank of England for seventeen years as a monetary adviser, becoming a Chief Adviser in 1980. In 1997 he was appointed one of the outside independent members of the Bank of England's new Monetary Policy Committee until May 2000. Earlier he had taught at Cambridge and LSE.

Besides numerous articles, he has written a couple of books on monetary history; a graduate monetary textbook, *Money, Information and Uncertainty* (2nd Ed. 1989); two collections of papers on monetary policy, *Monetary Theory and Practice* (1984) and *The Central Bank and The Financial System* (1995); and a number of books and articles on Financial Stability, on which subject he was Adviser to the Governor of the Bank of England, 2002-2004, and numerous other studies relating to financial markets and to monetary policy and history.

Andrew Crockett is President of JPMorgan Chase International, and a member of the Executive Committee of JPMorgan Chase & Co. Before joining JPMorgan Chase, Mr. Crockett had been General Manager (CEO) of the Bank for

International Settlements ('The Central Banks' Bank'), serving two five-year terms. At the request of the G-7 Finance Ministers, he also served from 1999-2003 as the first Chairman of the Financial Stability Forum, a group of senior financial officials from the major economies that monitors the health of the International Financial System. Earlier in his career, Mr. Crockett had held senior positions at the Bank of England and the International Monetary Fund.

Mr. Crockett has also served in the past as Chairman of Working Party 3 of the OECD, as Alternate Governor of the IMF for the United Kingdom, as a member of the Monetary Committee of the European Union; and as a Trustee of the International Accounting Standards Committee Foundation. He is currently a member of the Group of 30, Chairman of the Per Jacobsson Foundation, member of the International Council of the China Banking Regulatory Commission, member of the International Council of the China Development Bank, Director of the International Centre for Leadership in Finance (Malaysia), and a trustee of the American University of Beirut.

Among honours received by Mr. Crockett are Honorary LLD (University of Birmingham) European Banker of the year (2000), and Knight Bachelor (United Kingdom, 2003). He is the author of several books on economic and financial subjects, as well as numerous articles in scholarly publications.

Avinash Persaud's career spans finance, academia and policy advice. He was a top ranked sell-side analyst for 15 years and a senior executive at State Street, J. P. Morgan and UBS GAM before becoming Chairman of Intelligence Capital Limited in 2005, a financial advisory boutique. He won the Jacques de Larosiere Prize from the IIF in 2000 for his essay 'Sending the herd off the cliff edge' on how trends in risk management and regulation were leading to systemic risks.

He is an Emeritus Professor of Gresham College and Visiting Fellow at CFAP, Judge Institute, Cambridge. He was elected a Member of Council of the Royal Economics Society (2007), is a Governor and former Member of Council of the London School of Economics. Persaud is known for his work on 'liquidity black holes' and investors' shifting risk appetite.

Persaud is a Member of the UN Commission of Experts on International Financial Reform, Chairman of the Second Warwick Commission, Co-Chair of the OECD EmNet, Deputy Chair of the Overseas Development Institute and one of the founding directors of the Global Association of Risk Professionals (2002-2009). He was formerly a Visiting Scholar at the IMF (2001) and the European Central Bank (2006).

Hyun Song Shin is the Hughes-Rogers Professor of Economics at Princeton University, affiliated with the Department of Economics and the Bendheim Center for Finance. Prior to coming to Princeton, he was Professor of Finance at the London School of Economics. Professor Shin's current research is on financial economics and economic theory with particular reference to financial crises, disclosures, risk and financial stability issues, topics on which he has published widely both in academic and practitioner outlets. He has served as editor or editorial board member of several scholarly journals, and has served in an advisory capacity to central banks and policy organizations on financial stability issues. He is a fellow of the Econometric Society and of the British Academy.

Contents

List of Tables

List of Figures

List of Boxes

List of Conference Participants

Edmond Alphandéry	Chairman of the Board, CNP Assurances, Paris
Svein Andresen	Secretary General, Financial Stability Forum, Basel
Richard Apostolik	President & CEO, Global Association of Risk Professionals, London
Leszek Balcerowicz	Professor, Warsaw School of Economics, Warsaw
Richard Baldwin	Professor, The Graduate Institute of International and Development Studies, Geneva
Vit Barta	Adviser to the Vice Governor, Czech National Bank, Prague
Eric Barthalon	Executive Director/Head of TAA & Capital Markets, Allianz Investment Management-Allianz SE, Munich
Rémy Bersier	CEO Private Banking, Head of French speaking markets, Bank Julius Bär, Geneva
Robert Bichsel	Deputy Head, Financial Stability Unit, Swiss National Bank, Zürich
Niklaus Blattner	Emeritus professor of economics, University of Basel, Basel
Jürg Blum	Deputy Head of Financial Stability, Swiss National Bank, Bern
Laurence Boone	Chief Economist (France), Barclays Capital, Paris
Claudio Borio	Head of Research and Policy Analysis, Bank for International Settlements, Basel
Markus Brunnermeier	Edwards S. Sanford Professor of Economics, Princeton University, Princeton
Mark Carey	Adviser International Finance,

	Federal Reserve Board, Washington DC
Stephen Cecchetti	Economic Adviser and Head of the Monetary and Economic Department, Bank for International Settlements, Basel
Benoit Coeuré	Head of Multilateral and Development Affairs, Ministry of Finance, Paris
Jean-Pierre Danthine	Professor, University of Lausanne Managing Director, Swiss Finance Institute, Lausanne
Pierre Darier	Partner, Lombard Odier Darier Hentsch & Cie, Geneva
José De Grégorio	Governor, Central Bank of Chile, Santiago
Jacques Delpla	Member, Council of Advisers to the Prime Minister, Paris
Paul Dembinski	Director, Observatoire de la Finance, Geneva
Godfried De Vidts	Director of European Affairs, ICA, London
Christian Donze	Managing Director/Head of Southern Europe, Deutsche Bank, Geneva
Marc Flandreau	Professor, The Graduate Institute, Geneva
Paolo Garonna	Deputy Executive Secretary, UN Economic Commission for Europe, Geneva
Stefan Gerlach	Professor of Monetary Economics, Institute for Monetary and Financial Stability, Goethe University of Frankfurt, Frankfurt
Michel Girardin	Member of Senior Management, Union Bancaire Privée, Geneva
Charles Goodhart	Norman Sosnow Professor of Banking and Finance, London School of Economics, London
David Green	Advisor of International Affairs, Financial Reporting Council, London
Daniel Heller	Director of Financial Systems, Swiss National Bank, Bern
Anne Héritier Lachat	Member of the Board, FINMA, Swiss Financial Markets Supervisory Authority, Geneva
Richard Herring	Jacob Safra Professor of International Banking and Professor of Finance, The Wharton School, University of Pennsylvania,

	Philadelphia
Philipp Hildebrand	Vice-Chairman of the Governing Board, Swiss National Bank, Bern
Sir Christopher Hogg	Chairman, Financial Reporting Council, London
Stefan Ingves	Governor, Sveriges Riksbank, Stockholm
Nigel Jenkinson	Adviser Governors & Secretaries, Bank of England, London
Manuel Jetzer	Managing Director, Credit Suisse, Geneva
Kerstin af Jochnick	Chair CEBS, Committe af European Banking Supervisors, Stockholm
Thomas Jordan	Member of the Governing Board, Swiss National Bank, Zürich
Edward Kane	James F. Cleary Professor in Finance, Boston College, Boston
Pierre Keller	Former Senior Partner, Lombard Odier Darier Hentsch & Cie, Geneva
Ulrich Kohli	Alternate Member of the Governing Board, Swiss National Bank, Zürich
Jean-Pierre Landau	Deputy Governor, Banque de France, Paris
David Longworth	Deputy Governor, Bank of Canada, Ottawa
Henri Loubergé	Professor of Economics, University of Geneva, Geneva
Stan Maes	Member of The Chief Economist Team, European Commission, Brussels
Sylvie Matherat	Director Financial Stability, Banque de France, Paris
Maurice Monbaron	Vice Chairman of the Board of Directors, Crédit Agricole (Suisse) SA, Geneva
Jonas Niemeyer	Head of Policy and Analysis Division, Sveriges Riksbank, Stockholm
John Nugee	Managing Director, Official Institutions Group, State Street Global Advisors, London
Danièle Nouy	Secretary General, Commission Bancaire, Paris
Ugo Panizza	Unit Chief Debt and Finance Analysis, UNCTAD, Geneva

Lucas Papademos	Vice President, European Central Bank, Frankfurt
Avinash Persaud	Chairman, Intelligence Capital Limited & Investment, London
Michel Peytrignet	Head, Economic Affairs, Swiss National Bank, Zürich
Jean Pisani-Ferry	Director, Bruegel, Brussels
Richard Portes	President, Center for Economic Policy Research, London Professor of Economics, London Business School, London
Hermann Remsperger	Member of the Executive Board, Deutsche Bundesbank, Frankfurt
Rafael Repullo	Professor of Economics, CEMFI, Madrid
Robert Reoch	Director, New College Capital Ltd, London
Bertrand Rime	Head of Financial Stability, Swiss National Bank, Bern
Alain Robert	Head Wealth Management & Business Banking Switzerland, UBS AG, Zürich
Märten Ross	Deputy Governor and Member of the Executive Board, Bank of Estonia, Tallinn
Salvatore Rossi	Managing Director, Economic Research and International Relations, Banca d'Italia, Rome
Claudio Segré	Chairman, Argus fund, SEFI SA, Geneva
Dirk Schoenmaker	Professor, Free University of Amsterdam, Amsterdam
Robert Shelburne	Chief Economist, UN Economic Commission for Europe, Geneva
Hyun Shin	Professor of Economics, Princeton University, Princeton
Frank Smets	Managing Director – Research, European Central Bank, Frankfurt
David Strachan	Director Financial Stability Division, Financial Services Authority, London
Alexander Swoboda	Professor, International Economics, The Graduate Institut, Geneva

Istvan-Pal Szekely	Research Director, DG Ecfin, European Commission, Brussels
Cédric Tille	Professor, The Graduate Institute, Geneva
Paul Tucker	Executive Director-Markets, Bank of England, London
Gertrude Tumpel-Gugerell	Member of the Executive Board, European Central Bank, Frankfurt
Angel Ubide	Director of Global Economics, Tudor Investment Corporation, Washington DC
Silvina Vatnick	President, Center for Financial Stability, Buenos Aires
José Viñals	Deputy Governor, Banco de España, Madrid
Ignazio Visco	Member of the Board and Deputy Director General, Banca d'Italia, Rome
Sushil Wadhwani	Director, Wadhwani Asset Management, London
Beatrice Weder Di Mauro	Professor of Economics, University of Mainz German Council of Economic Experts
Bill White	Previous Economic Adviser and Head of the Monetary and Economic Department, Bank for International Settlements, Basel
Sir Nigel Wicks	Chairman, Euroclear, London
Thomas Wiedmer	Alternate Member of the Governing Board, Department II, Swiss National Bank, Bern
Jonathan Wilmot	Managing Director, Global Strategy, Fixed Income Research, Crédit Suisse, London
Pawel Wyczanski	Advisor, Financial System, National Bank of Poland, Warsaw
Charles Wyplosz	Professor, International Economics, The Graduate Institute, Geneva Director, ICMB, Geneva

Acknowledgements

The authors wish to thank Viral Acharya, Tobias Adrian, Kern Alexander, Ing-Haw Cheng, Douglas Diamond, John Eatwell, Michael Foot, Geoffrey Gardiner, Philipp Hartmann, Richard Johnson, Anil Kashyap, Jean-Pierre Landau, Stephen Morris, Maria Nieto, John Nugee, Martin Oehmke, John Pattison, Enrico Perotti, Richard Portes, Brian Quinn, Raghuram Rajan, Robert Reoch, Rafael Repullo, Martin Schmalz, Anil Shamdasani, Steve Thieke, John Walsh, John Williamson, Charles Wyplosz and Tanju Yorulmazer.

Any views expressed are those of the authors and should not be regarded as those of the institutions with which they are affiliated.

Foreword

Today's financial regulatory systems assume that regulations which make individual banks safe also make the financial system safe. The eleventh *Geneva Report on the World Economy* shows that this thinking is flawed. Actions that banks take to make themselves safer can – in times of crisis – undermine the system's stability. The Report argues for a different approach.

The Report builds on its predecessor, the ninth *Geneva* Report, which examined the main threats to financial stability in the global economy. The initial version of the ninth Report was presented at a conference in May 2007, before the crisis had emerged. The Report's authors were far from sanguine even then, and the discussions at the conference focused on the fault lines in the global financial system. The Report was published in November 2007, when these fault lines had become apparent and turmoil in financial markets had already claimed its first victim, Northern Rock.

In the year that followed, first global financial markets and then the global economy deteriorated, at first gradually, and then with alarming speed. By late 2008 it was apparent that the policy prescriptions in the ninth Report did not go nearly far enough, given the severity of the problems facing policy-makers. ICMB therefore brought forward the eleventh Report, which was presented at a conference in January 2009 and was widely circulated in draft form at that time. The Report does indeed, as hoped, address the fundamental issues that lie at the heart of the difficulties facing the global financial system and its regulators.

As Mervyn King has rightly said, 'The costs of this crisis are not to be measured simply in terms of its impact on public finances, the destruction of wealth and the number of jobs lost. They are also to be seen in the lost trust in the financial sector among other parts of our economy ...' ICMB and CEPR are delighted to provide a forum for the authors to put forward this careful analysis of financial regulation. The measures they propose, by improving the functioning of global financial markets, would go some way toward restoring this trust.

Charles Wyplosz
Stephen Yeo

25 June 2009

Executive Summary

There is a widespread view that the Credit Crunch of 2007-9 was, in part, a result of insufficient reach of regulation and that a solution is to take existing regulation and spread it more comprehensively across more institutions and jurisdictions. That would be an incorrect diagnosis. At the heart of the crisis were highly regulated institutions in regulated jurisdictions. The crisis has involved a regulatory failure as much as anything else. Our solution is not more regulation per se, though that may well be required in some areas, but better and different regulation. This is not the first banking crisis that the world has seen. It is more likely to be nearer the one hundredth. If crises keep repeating themselves, policy should change. But it also means that policy makers should not superficially over-react to the particular characters and colour of the current crisis. Schadenfreude at bankers' expense is satisfying, but it does not really get us anywhere. The crisis should be a call to remedy fundamental market failures that have either been ignored or improperly dealt with in our regulation so far.

Systemic risks

It is perhaps banal by now to point out that the reason why we try to prevent banking crises is that the costs to society are invariably enormous and exceed the private cost to individual financial institutions. We regulate in order to internalize these externalities. The main tool which regulators use to do so, is capital adequacy requirements, but the current approach has been found wanting. It implicitly assumes that we can make the system as a whole safe by simply trying to make sure that individual banks are safe. This sounds like a truism, but in practice it represents a fallacy of composition. In trying to make themselves safer, banks, and other highly leveraged financial intermediaries, can behave in a way that collectively undermines the system.

Selling an asset when perceived risk increases, is a prudent response from the perspective of an individual bank. But if many banks act in this way, the asset price will collapse, forcing institutions to take yet further steps to rectify the situation. Such responses by banks lead to generalised declines in asset prices, and to enhanced correlations and volatility in asset markets. Risk is endogenous to bank behaviour.

Through a number of avenues, some regulatory, some not, often in the name of sophistication, transparency and modernity, the increasing role of current market prices on behaviour has intensified such endogeneity. These avenues include mark-to-market valuation of assets; regulatory approved market-based measures of risk, such as credit default swap spreads in internal credit models or price volatility in market risk models; and the increasing use of credit ratings, which tend to be correlated, directionally at least, with market prices.

Risk and the economic cycle

In the up-phase of an economic cycle, price-based measures of asset values rise, volatility-based measures of risk fall, and competition to grow bank profits increases. Most financial institutions spontaneously respond by (i) expanding their balance sheets; (ii) trying to lower the cost of funding by using short-term funding from the money markets; and (iii) increasing leverage. Those that do not do so are seen as underleveraging their equity and are punished by the stock markets. Market discipline does not operate in booms.

When the boom ends, asset prices fall and short-term funding to institutions with impaired and uncertain assets or high leverage dries up. Forced sales of assets drive up their measured risk and, invariably, the boom turns to bust. At that point markets want banks to have ever more capital, further turning the downwards screw.

The current approach to banking regulation seems to assume that financial crashes occur randomly as a result of a bad institution failing and then the failure becoming systemic. In reality, crashes follow booms. The current crisis is yet another instance of an all too familiar boom and bust cycle. But if crises repeat themselves - following a boom-bust cycle - banning the products, players and jurisdictions that were circumstantially at the centre of the current crisis will do little to prevent the next one. Instead we need to supplement micro-prudential regulation with macro-prudential regulation to calm the booms and soften the busts.

Micro and macro-prudential regulation

Micro prudential regulation concerns itself with the stability of each individual institution. Macro-prudential regulation concerns itself with the stability of the financial system as a whole. Micro-prudential regulation examines the responses of an individual bank to exogenous risks. By construction it does not incorporate endogenous risk. It also ignores the systemic importance of individual institutions depending on such factors as size, degree of leverage and interconnectedness with the rest of the system.

One of the key purposes of macro-regulation is to act as a countervailing force to the natural decline in measured risks in a boom and the subsequent rise in measured risks in the subsequent collapse. This has to be rule-based, or at least supervisory discretion needs to be more constrained. Supervisors currently have plenty of discretion, but they find it hard to utilize it because of the politics of booms when all seems well, and lenders, borrowers, politicians and the media are all basking in the rosy glow of apparent success.

At the centre of this Geneva Report is the proposal to make capital requirements counter-cyclical. In practical terms we recommend regulators increase the existing capital adequacy requirements (based on an assessment of inherent risks) by one, or perhaps two, multiples. We want to interact macro-prudential with micro-prudential regulations (essentially Basel II) for two main reasons, rather than abandoning Basel II altogether. First, micro-prudenital regulation remains valid and necessary; it is just insufficient on its own. Second, it is easier to manipulate (to 'game') each individual regulation on its own, than when they work together.

The first multiplier is related to above average growth of credit expansion and to leverage. Regulators and central bankers should agree on the degree of bank asset growth and leverage that is consistent with the long-run target for nominal GDP. The multiple on capital charges rises the more credit expansion exceeds this target. The purpose of this capital charge is not to eliminate the economic cycle, something which would require us to have an ability to forecast the cycle better than we can, but to lean against the wind and ensure that banks are putting aside an increasing amount of capital in an up-cycle when currently available risk measures would suggest that they can safely leverage more. This extra capital can then be released when the boom ends and asset prices fall back. The counter-cyclical charge should serve to moderate the boom-bust cycle.

The second multiple on capital charges could be related to the mismatch in the maturity of assets and liabilities. Alternatively the Central Bank could levy a varying premium for insuring against liquidity risk, again related to mismatch. One of the main lessons of the Crash of 2007/8 is that the risk of an asset is substantially influenced by the maturity of its funding. Northern Rock and other casualties of the crash might well have survived with the same assets if the average maturity of their funding had been longer. If regulators make little distinction on how assets are funded, financial institutions will rely on cheaper, short-term funding, which increases systemic fragility. This can be off-set through the imposition of a capital charge, or premium, that is inversely related to the maturity of funding of such assets as cannot normally be posted at the central bank for liquidity.

To further reduce the spiral of sales in a crisis and to support financial institutions in lengthening the maturity of their funding, we also propose that instead of suspending mark-to-market value accounting, financial institutions could complement mark-to-market accounting with mark-to-funding valuations, which would be more appropriate for assessing risk and capital adequacy.

Not all financial institutions are alike

Not all financial institutions pose similar systemic risks. Regulation should acknowledge that some banks are systemically important and the others are less so. We propose that, in each country, supervisors should determine, (but not publicise), which are the systemically-important institutions that need closer scrutiny and greater control.

All banks, and any other financial institution subject to deposit insurance, should also be subject to some (low) minimum capital requirement as a protection for the deposit insurance fund. Systemically-important institutions would be subject both to micro-prudential regulation and to macro-prudential regulation, related to their contribution to systemic risk. This can be done by adjusting the micro-prudential ratio by a coefficient corresponding to their macro-prudential risk.

A major chunk of bank lending consists of mortgages on housing and commercial property. The financial system is more closely intertwined with the property market than with, for example, the equity market. The concurrent cycle in the housing market was exacerbated by procyclical swings in loan terms, such as loan-to-value and loan-to-income ratios. We advocate that this be stopped and, even perhaps, reversed.

However, we do not share the zeal of some for governments to be involved in the decisions of private firms in matters of executive compensation at systemically important institutions. While not ruling out particular measures to lengthen bankers' horizons, we hope that macro-prudential regulation will push banks to develop incentive packages that encourage longer-term behaviour. If that failed, regulators could do more. Incentives are important.

Global arrangements for global banks

Another common view is that financial institutions are global and so financial regulation needs to be global. This is poetic, but the disharmonious reality is that more international meetings would not have averted the crisis and the crisis has taught us that there is much we need to do at the national level to strengthen regulation. Counter-cyclical charges and charges for liquidity cannot be implemented or set globally but need to be done nationally. There is a clear need for information sharing and co-ordination of the *principles* of regulatory actions, but in the actual application of (internationally agreed) principles of rules and supervision, we recommend a switch back from 'home country' regulation towards 'host country' regulation. We believe this could have two further benefits. First, if foreign banks were required to set up their local presence as independent subsidiaries that might withstand the default of an international parent, it would reduce exposure to lax jurisdictions more effectively than trying to force all to follow a standard that would likely be inappropriate to many. Second, while this may seem counter to the thrust of European initiatives, nationally-based counter-cyclical charges could give the euro area (or any other common-currency area, formal or otherwise) a much needed additional policy instrument that could provide a more differentiated response, than a single interest rate can, to an (asset price) boom in one member state and stagflation in another.

Final word

The previous focus on micro-prudential regulation needs to be supplemented by macro-prudential regulation. While we cannot hope to prevent crises completely, we can perhaps make them fewer and milder by adopting and implementing better regulation.

Introduction

The authors of this *Geneva Report on the World Economy* are predominantly macro and finance economists. In our view such economic analysis and insight has, in the past, been insufficiently applied to the design of financial regulation. The purpose of this paper is to help rectify that lacuna.

The crisis which began in the US sub-prime mortgage market in early 2007 and then spread broadly and deeply was not the first banking crisis. It was closer to the 100th. We can draw a few important implications from this observation. If an event with widespread and severe economic and social consequences keeps on repeating itself, the onus is surely on the authorities to change something. Chiding bankers is satisfying; but insufficient. When a regulatory mechanism has failed to mitigate boom/bust cycles, simply reinforcing its basic structure is not likely to be a successful strategy. Moreover, a type of crisis that repeats itself cannot easily be put down to new, complex, instruments. In this report, we set our sights on moderating the recurring cycle of financial crises, cycles that in our view are not wedded to particular instruments, institutions, individuals or information.

The prevention of crises in the banking system is more important than in the case of other industries. As outlined in Chapter 1, the externalities from an individual bank failure both to other banks and thence to the wider economy are just so much greater. One of the key purposes of bank regulation is to internalize the social costs of potential bank failures via capital adequacy requirements. The regulation of banks must do more than instil best practice amongst bankers, or converge regulatory capital to the capital a prudential bank would otherwise hold. The current approach to systemic regulation implicitly assumes that we can make the system as a whole safe by simply trying to make sure that individual banks are safe. This sounds like a truism, but in practice it represents a fallacy of composition. In trying to make themselves safer, banks, and other highly leveraged financial intermediaries, can behave in a way that collectively undermines the system. Selling an asset when the price of risk increases, is a prudent response from the perspective of an individual bank. But if many banks act in this way, the asset price will collapse, forcing institutions to take yet further steps to rectify the situation. It is, in part, the responses of the banks themselves to such pressures that leads to generalised declines in asset prices, and enhanced correlations and volatility in asset markets. Such endogeneity of risk, described further in Chapter 2, is greater the more there is a common driver of behaviour.

Financial crashes do not occur randomly, but generally follow booms. Through a number of avenues, some regulatory, some not, though often in the name of risk-sensitivity, sophistication and modernity, the role of current market prices on behaviour has intensified. These avenues include mark-to-market valuation of assets; regulatory approved market-based measures of risk, such as credit default swap spreads in internal credit models or price volatility in market risk models; and the increasing use of credit ratings, which tend to be correlated, directionally at least, with market prices.

In the up-phase of the economic cycle, price-based measures of asset values rise, price-based measures of risk fall and competition to grow bank profits increases. Market discipline encourages financial institutions to respond to these three related developments by some combination of (i) expanding their balance sheets to take advantage of the fixed costs of banking franchises and regulation (ii) trying to lower the cost of funding by using short-term funding from the money markets and (iii) increasing leverage. Those that do not do so are seen as underutilizing their equity and are punished by the stock markets. When the boom ends, and asset prices fall and short-term funding to institutions with impaired and uncertain assets or high leverage dries up, leading to forced sales of assets which drives up their measured risk, the boom turns to bust.

In Chapter 3, we distinguish between micro and macro-prudential regulation.[1] Micro prudential regulation concerns itself with factors that affect the stability of individual institutions. Macro-prudential regulation concerns itself with factors that affect the stability of the financial system as a whole. As we will attempt to show, the nature of the regulation applied to an individual financial institution depends crucially on how ' systemic' its activities are. This in turn is related, inter alia, to its size, degree of leverage and interconnectedness with the rest of the system.

A critical component of macro-prudential regulation must be to act as a countervailing force to the natural decline in measured risks in a boom and the subsequent rise in measured risks in the subsequent collapse. This countervailing force has to be as much rule based as possible. Supervisors have plenty of discretion, but their ability to utilize it is limited by the general short-sighted desire to prolong a boom and by bankers pleading for equality of treatment. In a boom, lending, leverage and reliance on short-term liquidity become mutually reinforcing and excessive. To counter this we propose, in Chapter 4, counter-cyclical capital charges. Regulators should increase the existing capital adequacy requirements (based on an assessment of inherent risks) by two multiples. The first is related to above average growth of credit expansion and leverage. Regulators should agree on the degree of bank asset growth and leverage that is consistent with the long-run target for nominal GDP, so that the multiple on capital charges rises the more credit expansion exceeds this target. The purpose of this capital charge is not to eliminate the economic cycle – something which would be unrealistically ambitious – but to ensure that in a boom, when risk measures are suggesting banks can safely leverage or lend more, banks are putting aside an increasing amount of capital which can then be released when the boom ends and asset prices fall back.

The second multiple on capital charges should be related to the mis-match in the maturity of assets and liabilities, as discussed in Chapter 5. One of the significant lessons of the Crash of 2007/8 is that the risk of an asset is largely deter-

1 Crockett (2000) was, perhaps, the first to draw this distinction.

mined by the maturity of its funding. Our proposed adjustment to mark-to-market accounting should provide a further incentive to reduce maturity mismatch. Northern Rock and other casualties of the crash might well have survived with the same assets, if the average maturity of their funding had been longer. When regulators make little distinction how assets are funded, there is a tendency for financial institutions to rely on cheaper, short-term funding, which increases systemic fragility. If short-term funding of long-term assets carries a capital cost – because it weighs on systemic stability – it will moderate banks' reliance on systemically adverse short-term funding and encourage them to seek longer-term funding.

A combination of these charges should push banks to develop incentive packages that are more encouraging of longer-term behaviour, as we outline in Chapter 6. A little more is required on this front, though we do not share the zeal of some for governments to be involved in the micro-decisions of private firms.

There is a tendency, commonly observed amongst politicians, to review the structure of the regulatory system before considering the potential instruments to achieve better regulatory control. Our position, Chapter 7, is the reverse. The structure of regulation should reflect the purposes and powers of the regulatory authorities. Macro-prudential, and micro-prudential, instruments are both needed, but differ in focus and in their needed professionalism. Hence, they should be carried out separately, respectively by Central Banks and by Financial Services Authorities. Again, financial and asset-price cycles differ from country to country. So contra-cyclical policy needs to be assumed more by the host country, thereby shifting some of the emphasis in regulation from the home to the host country.

Besides our key recommendations on macro-prudential measures and mark-to-funding, we make proposals on a whole series of minor issues, such as the role of stress tests, the adoption of maximum loan-to-value ratios in mortgage markets, etc., etc. These are gathered up and reported in our conclusion, Chapter 8. Really busy readers could skip straight there. Overall our intention is to develop a program of practical initiatives that could better attack the key features of externalities and systemic failure in financial markets.

1 Analytical Background

There is a vast body of financial regulation in existence. This is normally extended incrementally, frequently to close a loophole which some earlier fraud or financial disaster has exposed. Even such measures as may have seemed to involve a discrete jump in the regulatory process, such as the passage of the Basel I Accord in 1988, turn out, after closer inspection, to have been largely an attempt to agree on, and to harmonise, pre-existing 'best practices' in the key nation states, without much overt attempt to rationalise them against fundamental principles, or underlying theory. Exceptions occur only after major crises, as in the USA after 1929-33, (with Glass-Steagall and deposit insurance), and, perhaps, now.

There are good reasons for such an incremental approach under normal circumstances. Like the common law, it builds on the accrued wisdom of generations. It is practicable, do-able and (generally) common-sensical. Yet it is possible for such an incremental, and generally reactive, process to migrate over time in wrong, or just inferior, directions. When a major crisis erupts, such as that which has roiled financial systems in the world since August 2007, there is both a case and an opportunity for revisiting the underlying principles of (financial) regulation to examine whether the existing system is appropriately designed. There is a general willingness now to question existing regulatory practices and to consider, without prejudice, a wide range of alternative proposals. Nothing at this juncture is too hallowed by tradition and usage to escape questioning and to be off-limits to reform.[2] In particular, the regulatory system stands accused of having failed to

2 The temper of the times is illustrated by this passage from a paper by Davis, Polk and Wardwell, (the US law firm), to provide guidance on 'The Emergency Economic Stabilization Act of 2008', (October 4, 2008). They write, p. 43, that,

> "The Act is only the first step in the return to health for the US financial system. The idea of restructuring the archaic US financial regulatory system has been in the academic air for sometime and was recently also taken up by Treasury in its Blueprint, (The Department of the Treasury Blueprint for a Modernized Financial Regulatory Structure issued on March 31, 2008.) It should be clear to all by now that the fragmented nature of the current US regulatory system was a co-conspirator in the creation of the mess. None of this invalidates the critiques of those who have pointed out problems with the Sarbanes-Oxley Act and its impact on the competitiveness of the US capital markets. The problems are, in fact, larger than the false dichotomy between regulation and deregulation. They are worse than that. The problem is one of ineffective regulation leading to the wrong types of incentives within a fragmented regulatory structure that was unable to cope with new products and new circumstances in a changed world. What is needed is a complete reordering of the system, including both deregulation and re-regulation, depending upon which is more effective for the stability of the financial system, the competitiveness of the US capital markets and the economic health of the country. Naturally, there will be many interests to balance and the ability of our political leaders to make those changes cannot be assumed."

mitigate the recent cycle in leverage, credit expansion and housing prices. Nothing was done to tighten regulations (e.g. on capital, liquidity or remuneration) in the upswing, nor, until recently, to relax the pro-cyclical implications of the accounting/regulatory framework in the downturn. Regulation, in effect, provided little or no check, nor barrier, to the decisions taken by banks, and other financial operators, in their pursuit of (short-term) profit maximisation. It was not adapted to changes in the underlying vulnerabilities in the system as a whole, (as some of us had warned earlier, in Danielsson et al., 2001), and allowed financial engineering to avoid its impact, e.g. SIVs and other methods of deconsolidating risks.

What is needed is, first, a restatement of the basic objectives of financial regulation and, then, an assessment of whether the current regulatory framework is well structured to attain such objectives, and, if not, to explore what can be done to restructure such regulation so that it does.

So let us start by asking what should be the purposes of regulation. Traditional economic theory suggests that there are three main purposes.

1. to constrain the use of monopoly power and the prevention of serious distortions to competition and the maintenance of market integrity;
2. to protect the essential needs of ordinary people in cases where information is hard or costly to obtain, and mistakes could devastate welfare; and
3. where there are sufficient externalities that the social, and overall, costs of market failure exceed both the private costs of failure and the extra costs of regulation.

(1) above has been a main rationale for the regulation of private utilities, but, until recently,[3] has only entered the financial scene in a few rare cases, e.g. where the network economies of having a single market procedure, e.g. a clearing house, are so great that those who control access to the network could potentially extort huge rents from those trying to join.

The effect of the recent crisis, as it was also in Japan, has, however, been to reduce competition in the banking industry. In order to prevent weaker banks from failing, they have been folded into stronger, and generally larger, banks, thereby creating a small number of national 'champions' in each country.[4] Japanese City banks have been reduced to three. JPMorgan Chase, Bank of

---

3 The 10% limit for deposit concentration in the USA could soon become relevant.

4 The Daily Telegraph, October 1, 2008. Our thanks are due to Russell Taylor, writer of the Alex Cartoon, for permission to reprint this.

America, Wells Fargo/Wachovia and Citibank now bestride the US scene, (though all remain nominally subject to the 10% deposit cap). Concerns about reductions in competition are brushed aside, as with the Lloyds/HBOS merger, in the rush to shore up a fragile system. The result is an oligopolistic system, dominated by 'champions' who are far too large to fail, in some smaller countries (e.g. Iceland) perhaps too large to save, and are in a position to wield great influence and power.

How serious are the dangers posed by such greater concentration? Some banking markets have become more contestable, notably via IT techniques, such as bidding for time deposits; others are less so, e.g. loans to SMEs. Our proposals may very slightly mitigate the trend towards concentration by proposing tougher regulation for large, systemic banks. Beyond that, however, we advocate reinforced scrutiny by the competition authorities of potential anti-competitive practice by the larger banks. We are, however, aware that this is a larger and more difficult issue than we have been able to tackle in this monograph.

(2) above has come to mean that bank deposits have become implicitly, or explicitly, fully (100%) insured and guaranteed, at least up to some upper limit. This has now gone further in the current crisis. By the same token there are controls on the behaviour of insurance companies and pension funds. Mutual funds, unit trusts, money market funds, etc., are not guaranteed except in extreme cases, such as recently observed in the USA, but are required to behave in certain required ways. The debate in these cases is not whether they should be regulated, but how this might best be done. The point is that the political process works to protect the interest of small (and sometimes large) clients of financial institutions, regardless of the formal legal position. This is not going to change.

Such 100% deposit insurance, up to a now more elevated ceiling, creates moral hazard, both amongst depositors, and also amongst banks, so long as the premium paid by each bank is not accurately and immediately adjusted in alignment with such a bank's riskiness, (and this is difficult to apply, though the Canadian deposit insurance corporation, CDIC, has made a successful attempt along such lines). However awful, and risky, such a bank may be, or may become, it can always raise extra funds, once 100% insured, by raising interest rates slightly, (until and unless the supervisors close it down). In order to prevent the worst excesses of moral hazard, and to protect the tax payer, there is a need for a *minimum* level of capital, which, if breached, acts as a trigger for prompt corrective action (PCA). Such a minimum level of capital does not provide any protection for the shareholders and bank officers, rather the reverse as it is an intentional hostage, giving them necessary 'skin in the game'. Nor does it provide any resilience to the banking system, (only the buffer above such a minimum provides that), except in so far as PCA allows for an orderly run-down, rather than distressed sales and a news-worthy bankruptcy, of a bank in severe difficulties.

As has been clearly seen in 2007/8, (3) is by far the most important reason why banks, and certain other key financial intermediaries and markets, need regulation. But why does the failure of banks, and of some other financial institutions, involve systemic externalities that are not present when an ordinary manufacturing or service-sector firm goes bust. The basic answer comes from the fact that the failure of a banking-type institution, say Lehman Bros, Northern Rock or Glitnir, weakens the other banks and financial markets with which they were involved, whereas the failure of, say, a car company or a laundry tends to strengthen the remaining companies in the same sector, by removing a competitor. And lying behind this is the even more important consideration that the continued health of the financial system, and even more so of the banking sector within it, is key to the satisfactory functioning of the wider economy, to a qualitatively different extent from most other sectors.

There are, at least, five reasons for such negative externalities. The first is pure informational contagion, particularly in the context of intermediaries with a maturity mismatch between liabilities and assets (see Chapter 5). If bank A fails, this throws more doubt on the continued solvency of bank B, when B is perceived as being of the same type as A. When such doubt arises, depositors and lenders to B lose confidence, withdraw their funds, causing a sudden liquidity problem for B; this moves relative interest rates, and access to funds, against B, making its future solvency even more threatened. Thus the failure of Lehman Bros rapidly led to the end of the US Securities House model, (with Merrill Lynch being forced into a merger with Bank of America, and Goldman Sachs and Morgan Stanley becoming banks). If Northern Rock had been allowed to fail, there might have been runs on Bradford and Bingley and on Alliance and Leicester the next day, and on HBOS on the following day.[5] The demise of Glitnir in Iceland was rapidly translated into the collapse of Landsbanki and Kaupthing. These last two examples, however, indicate that while the size of the bank in difficulties plays a role in the spread of resulting contagion, it is not the only factor. If the failing bank is (perceived as) similar to other banks, and the cause of its failure may apply to them also, then like Northern Rock and Glitnir it will be contagious. If, however, it is perceived as being a unique outlier (e.g. BCCI), or if the cause of loss is particular to that bank, and not applicable to its close competitors, (notably when arising from fraud, e.g. Barings and Nick Leeson, Soc Gen and Jerome Kerviel), then there is much less risk of direct contagion.

But will not the same argument apply to other non-bank companies? If car producer A fails, it is likely to be due to a generalised fall in demand for cars. Will not this lead lenders to car producer B, whether on commercial paper, trade credit and bonds to refuse to renew or roll over, even despite the greater demand for B's products? The failure of the car company, however, does not have such an important signalling effect for its competitors. If the demand for cars falls, this is evident to lenders well before the first company fails. The failure of one car company means that the remaining companies will do better, not worse.[6] Moreover, most corporates and many households have a contingent line of credit with their bank, to tide them over such difficulties, until they can restore their own position by cutting cost, or increasing profits on sales, after their competitor's failure. So non-banks rely on banks in a crisis, while banks in turn have to rely on the Central Bank.

This leads on to the reason for the second externality arising from bank failures, which is a loss of access to future funding for the failed bank's customers. Of course, a client of failed bank A can try to transfer her custom to surviving bank B, but bank B will have less direct information on this client, and is likely, espe-

5 While the cynical will note that such runs were only delayed by a few quarters, the breathing space gained might have allowed the crisis to be resolved with much less loss.

6 GM, however, has argued that if there should be common suppliers, then its failure could adversely rebound on Ford and Chrysler by causing the bankruptcy of such suppliers.

cially in the likely conditions of fear and panic surrounding major instances of bank failure, only to provide replacement credit facilities on much tougher terms. A bank failure causes an externality in the guise of the loss of specific information links between the failed bank and its customers. While this is also the case in other industries which have long-term relationships with their customers, it is especially pronounced for banks.

The third externality is that banks, and financial intermediaries, trade much more amongst themselves than do other corporates. Hotels and steel mills do not have significant inter-hotel or inter-furnace markets. Such interactions between banks and other financial intermediaries relate not only to the straight-forward interbank market, but also to an increasing range of other derivative markets, involving guarantees (mono-line insurers), credit default swaps, as well as prime brokerage services, etc., etc. It was because of the ramifications of such connections that both Bear Stearns and AIG were provided with public sector support, and, in part, because of such ramifications that the failure of Lehman Bros proved so devastating.[7]

In the longer run when the dust has settled, a failing bank (like Continental Illinois) can often pay back a large percentage of its inter-bank borrowing, and the need to rearrange derivative contracts, to which the failed bank was a party, can ultimately come out close to a zero-sum game. But in the immediate aftermath of the failure of an inter-connected bank, there is much uncertainty about how much creditors of that bank will get back, and by what date. This will lead analysts to try to make instant assessments of who potentially stands most at risk, and this will then feed directly back to our first externality, informational contagion. Thus the fact that Continental Illinois did ultimately pay back to its correspondent banks over 90 cents in the dollar is *not* proof that its (abrupt and disorderly) failure might not have triggered runs on at least some of its correspondent banks.

So far we have been concerned only with the failures of banks, and some other systemic institutions. But that failure is generally triggered by a decline in the value of the assets held by the bank, and by a run on the bank, itself usually primarily caused by a perceived decline in the bank's asset values. Liquidity problems usually generate underlying solvency worries, (though the illiquid bank will attempt to deny this, as in Northern Rock, the Icelandic banks, etc.). In order to deal with such liquidity problems prior to failure, and in the course of liquidation after failure, the bank in difficulties will often be forced to sell assets (fire sales). But such sales will drive down the current market price of the same assets held on other banks' books, when these are valued on a mark-to-market basis. And, of course, the same is true the other way around; solvency is not exogenous to liquidity. When there is a generalised liquidity problem attempts to deal with it will lead to declines in asset values, creating a solvency problem, even where none existed before. In short, there is an internal amplifying process (liquiditiy spirals) whereby a falling asset market leads banks, investment houses, etc., to make more sales (deleveraging), which further drives down asset prices and financial inter-

7 An additional related problem is the mutual impact of declines in the credit standing of counterparties. If bank A has an OTC claim on bank B, whose credit is downgraded, the net worth of bank A will decline, and vice versa. If both should occur simultaneously, then in pure mark-to-market accounting, there should be no change in net worth, as the value of each bank's liabilities has declined by the same amount as its assets, but it is artificial for a bank to take credit for the view that it is less likely to repay its liabilities.

mediaries' assessed profit and loss and balance sheet net worth.

We believe that it is this internal, self-amplifying dynamic that has lain at the root of both the recent, and virtually all prior, financial crises. The argumentation and analysis for this claim is set out at greater length in Chapter 2. Thus we believe that financial crises are predominantly caused by market dynamics, not just by external shocks, though such shocks, e.g. the downturn in the US housing market in 2006, the quadrupling of oil prices in 1973/74, the Stock Market collapse in 1929, may well have been the trigger.

One immediate implication of this is that the standard format of banking stress tests is fundamentally insufficient. These stress tests review the effect on each bank's profits and capital of some (historically-based) exogenous shock. But, if financial crises are primarily caused by endogenous risk, whereby the banks' reactions to such a trigger sets off an amplifying spiral, via declines in asset prices and reductions in credit expansion, such stress tests, focussing on exogenous risk, will miss out on the (more important) second, and higher, round effects. Attempts to adjust stress tests for endogenous risk have not yet borne much fruit. It may be that the best way to assess the implications of endogenous risk is via new endogenous 'Co-risk-measures' that measure the increase in overall risk after conditioning on the fact that one bank is in trouble (possibly for endogenous reasons). Another way to go is develop a model to explore the likely actions, reactions and interactions within the banking system, but that remains largely an exercise for the future, (though the papers of Goodhart, Sunirand and Tsomocos (e.g. 2004, 2006a and b) represent a start).

The fifth, and final, form of externality is akin to the fourth. Instead of, or as well as, selling financial assets to regain liquidity, and to improve capital ratios, a bank, or financial intermediary, may seek to restrict new credit extension, e.g. by rationing via higher margins/haircuts or by raising interest rates, or other costs, to borrowers. Such deleveraging, via credit restriction, will have the general effect of lowering output and prices, whether of goods, or services, or assets in the economy. This will raise the probability of default for all other borrowers. Thus there is yet a further self-amplifying spiral whereby credit restriction weakens the economy, which leads to more default and asset price declines, which causes yet more credit restrictions.

The implication of all this is that the appropriate regulatory concern, caused by externalities, lies with the impact of the difficulties of the individual financial intermediary, whether by failure or large-scale forced deleveraging, on the wider system. And, of course, market failures (in the guise of resource misallocations) also occur during the boom phase, with excessive credit expansion and investment in the 'bubble' assets. That is, in principle, separate from the risk management practices of the individual bank. The individual small depositor is protected by deposit insurance (where the insurance fund in turn requires a *minimum* capital ratio and prompt corrective action as safeguard).[8] For the rest, the riskiness of an individual bank, or any other financial intermediary, should properly remain

8 The historical record suggests that bank failures can occur quite suddenly without an observable prior steady decline in capital ratios. So the combination of PCA and a minimum capital ratio may not be enough to protect the deposit insurance fund, and hence the taxpayer. This is one of the arguments, discussed later in Chapter 3, for extending micro-prudential supervision beyond the ranks of large and system institutions.

the province of the bank's managers, owners and debt holders, subject to market discipline, *except* in so far as that institution's demise should impinge on the wider system, via spill-overs and externalities.

So, the first claim of this paper is that regulation has been excessively focussed on seeking to improve the behaviour and risk management practices of individual banks, too micro-prudential, for which we would assert that it has slight justification in the theory of regulation. By the same token it has been far too little focussed on wider systemic issues, insufficiently macro-prudential, where it does have a locus. By consciously seeking to make prudential capital move more closely in accord with banks' own choice of economic capital, regulation did too little to restrain bank expansion in the upswing, nor has it been able to provide any support against the current implosion of the system as a whole.

Let us take two key examples of the difference between the macro and the micro perspective. First let us consider liquidity. In one of his earlier papers, Hellwig (1995) considers a banking system consisting of *n* banks, where *n* is quite large. A demand deposit is placed with the first bank, which lends it on in the interbank market for one week to bank 2, which lends it on for two weeks to bank 3, and so on, until finally bank *n* gets an interbank deposit for *n*-1 weeks and lends it on to an end-user for *n* weeks. No bank has a serious maturity mis-match, but the system as a whole does. It could unravel quite quickly. What occurred in 2007/8 was just such an unravelling of wholesale financial markets. This experience shows that neither the system as a whole, nor individual banks, such as Northern Rock, can put their faith for maintaining liquidity in continued, unquestioned, access to wholesale markets on reasonable terms.

From an individual bank/micro perspective, it was reasonable and efficient for each bank to assume that, in normal times, they would have access to the wholesale money markets. Once some banks made this assumption, banks that did not do so were put at a competitive disadvantage. This was one of the forces behind the de-mutualisation of building societies and their evolution into banks, so that they could tap wholesale money markets. At a micro-level this was not viewed as increasing risk, but reducing it by providing alternative and more flexible sources of funding. But the exploitation of market access by almost all banks in normal times, increased the likelihood of disaster in abnormal times.

This then raises the key question of which parties should stand behind the system to provide access to liquidity in the case of a failure of markets to function adequately. There are four present candidates. The first candidate is the banks themselves. Market failure most often occurs (ignoring physical problems, such as computer failure) because of credit counterparty risk. Government debt, when denominated in that Government's own currency, has no such risk. Banks with ample quantities of government paper amongst their assets can withstand temporary liquidity problems. But this requires that banks carry large quantities of government paper – providing less room for private lending – or that the credit and liquidity problems are contained in scope and time.[9] Yet credit and liquidity problems have a way of running along far reaching fault lines. If we are to rely solely

9 Minimum liquidity, or cash ratios, are, of course, poor ideas since the assets satisfying that minimum cannot be used. Holding assets as a proportion of wholesale funding is better, but what is actually needed is a counter-cyclical measure. Goodhart (2009) suggests one such possibility; Perotti and Suarez (2009) another.

on the banks, and do not wish to have an overly repressed credit system, we would have to induce banks to behave in a much more conservative, risk averse way – probably more so than would be consistent with an innovative, dynamic economic system.

Second, there could be private insurance. For example, the credit counter-party risk of an asset, bought on the basis of whole-sale funding, could be insured by another financial intermediary, e.g. a mono-line insurer, via the CDS market, etc. The problem with this is that the overall risk is not eliminated but simply transferred and often concentrated in (insurance) intermediaries whose own position would be threatened by a major shock. The problems of AIG, mono-lines and Fannie and Freddie are cases in point. Moreover, as touched on above, risks that appear uncorrelated in normal times become highly correlated in stress situations. Indeed rather than relying more on private insurance, the lesson of the recent crash is that bodies *and markets* that purport to provide credit insurance need to be brought more directly into the macro-prudential net, and have their ability to take on and concentrate such risk more closely controlled.

Third, the Central Bank could become the market maker of last resort, to use Willem Buiter's apt phrase (Buiter and Sibert, 2007; Buiter, 2009). When markets dry up, the Central Bank, in some extended Special Liquidity Scheme, takes the assets off the hands of the banks. If banks are leery of lending to each other, the Central Bank interposes itself as the central clearing house, taking in deposits from surplus banks and lending to deficit banks. There is not that much difference between being a 'lender of last resort' in a primarily bank-based system and being a 'market-maker of last resort' in a predominantly capital market system. Both are subject to the same kind of 'runs', that call for official intervention. Of course, the Central Bank might suffer some loss, if conditions become really dire, but with the Government and Treasury behind it, it can always be recapitalised.[10] A greater concern than loss (we believe) is moral hazard. Should the Central Bank step in as market maker of last resort at the first whiff of difficulty, would that not lead the banks, and other financial intermediaries, to take on much more risk in normal times in the belief that they could unload it on the Central Bank in bad times?

The fourth of our candidates is the Government (Treasury) which could provide public sector insurance against credit counter-party risk. This has now been done on a wide scale, and was the essence of the Kotlikoff/Mehrling/Milne (2008) proposal that the government guarantees the highest grade mortgage-based securities against such risk, thereby transforming them effectively into public sector debt. The questions then obviously arise on what terms and on what occasions the public sector should provide such insurance, and the prior issue of moral hazard recurs.

So, there are four potential sources of protecting the financial system against the failure of wholesale financial markets and, hence, of illiquidity. These are: (1) the banks, and the other financial institutions, themselves; (2) private insurance ; (3) the Central Bank; (4) public insurance. The question to be determined is what weight should be placed on each.

In addition to the case of liquidity, a second example of the difference between macro and micro prudential behaviour relates to capital adequacy. Indeed one rea-

10 The ECB would be recapitalised by its constituent NCBs.

son why regulators paid little attention to the liquidity problems discussed above was from a belief that if a bank had 'adequate'[11] capital, then it could always raise extra funding on wholesale markets. The micro-prudential approach suggested a risk-weighted capital adequacy requirement, as has indeed been introduced under Basel I and II. Surely a bank holding AAA assets is safer than a bank holding BBB assets, and therefore needs to hold significantly less capital, as prudential backing. Obviously in one sense, but not in another. Regulatory capital is meant to be held against unexpected loss, and not against expected loss, which should be met by a higher interest rate spread. The rating (should) measure the *expected* probability of default, whereas what matters is the likelihood of migration (downwards) of the rating, and the loss of value should that occur. Assume that both banks have the same risk-weighted tier one ratios, with say a similar buffer of 2% above the 4% requirement (i.e. 6%),[12] *and* that the risk of downwards migration (of say two notches) is the same for both assets, (AAA and BBB). Then which bank has more systemic risk? The answer generally is the AAA bank. This is for three reasons. First, AAA assets (many of which are mortgage-based structured products) are truly systemic, in the sense that they only lose value in a system-wide crisis, whereas BBB assets generally incorporate considerable idiosyncratic (i.e. diversifiable) risk. Second, the mark-to-market decline in value from the (assumed equal) migration may well be greater. Third, the relationship between rating and CAR is curved, see Figure 1, so that an equivalent horizontal migration leads to a greater proportionate requirement for extra capital at the 'best' end. So, for a given equal migration and equal capital buffer, the AAA bank will find itself in greater difficulties than the BBB bank.

Figure 1 The relationship between credit ratings and capital adequancy requirements

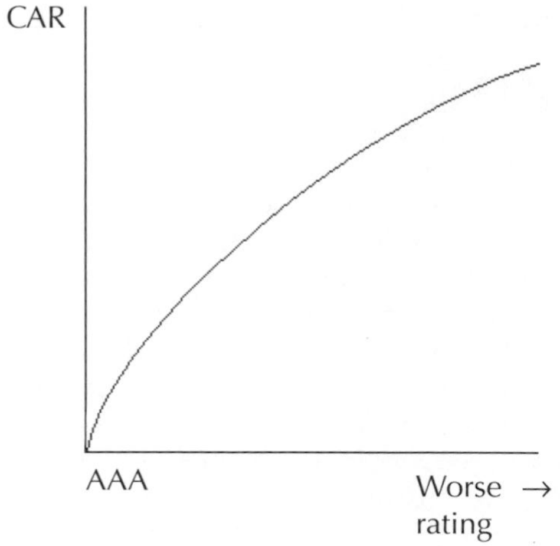

11 In some sense this depends on the definition of 'adequate'. What was regarded, in Basel I and II, as adequate clearly turned out not to be so, but with sufficiently high capital, (whatever that might be), this belief would have been better founded.

12 Having a minimum capital ratio, *as a protection for banks*, is just as silly as a minimum cash ratio, since it becomes unusable. We do advocate having such a minimum, but as a protection for the deposit insurer, and a trigger for prompt corrective action, and not in any way related to the need for resilience in the banking sector.

But perhaps this is no more than to record that risk-weightings are, inevitably flawed, and fail to reflect risk properly. More important is the point that micro-prudential measures, such as Basel II, and macro-prudential measures, such as we will advocate in Chapters 3 to 5, have differing purposes. The objective of a micro-prudential measure is to keep the individual institution behaving prudently, while that of the macro-prudential measure is to safeguard the system as a whole.

These two roles are often quite dissimilar. The micro-prudential concern is about individual risk; the macro-prudential with common, herd behaviour, and with shifts in generalised attitudes to risk. Individual institutional risk can often be seen to be low, or falling, as in 2004-6, when common macro-prudential risk is rising (and vice versa, as in 1992/93). Similarly, micro-prudential risk is concerned about risk concentration within individual institutions; macro-prudential-prudential risk relates more to similar portfolio holdings amongst institutions in the system. Indeed if all the individual institutions should be concentrated each in dissimilar portfolios (diversified into similar portfolios), the micro risk would be high, but the macro risk low (vice versa with low micro, but high macro risk). All this is set out in greater detail in Chapters 2 and 3.

Whereas we do claim that not enough attention has been given to macro-prudential risk alleviation, this is *not* to suggest that the present micro-prudential measures are unnecessary or wrongly designed (though they can be improved), but just insufficient on their own. Indeed where an institution, or market, is sufficiently large or strategic, so that its failure by itself would cause externalities, then it does need individually-targeted micro-prudential controls; in the case of banks this would be the Basel II risk-weighted CARs. Our point is rather that the micro-prudential regulations are not sufficient by themselves. They need to be supplemented by macro-prudential controls. We propose alternative measures whereby the Basel II risk-weighted CAR is interacted with macro-prudential measures to achieve a counter-cyclical overall effect and to penalise systemically dangerous funding mismatches. This issue, and the design of such counter-cyclical measures, is taken up in Chapter 4.

In principle, there are other routes whereby regulators can seek to make banks, and other relevant financial intermediaries, internalise the negative externalities that we have outlined. Besides capital charges, one could set a Pigovian tax on that activity, or try to provide insurance against contagious crises, either operated within the private sector, the public sector, or some combination of both. In practice banks will reckon that being forced to hold additional capital, counter-cyclically, is a form of taxation, when it bites; and capital charges have the additional advantage of providing protection to other stake-holders, including taxpayers.

We dismiss the possibility of purely private sector insurance, since this would just lead to the need for the government to protect the insurers (e.g. AIG). There have, however, been a number of proposals for some mixture of public and private insurance, usually on the grounds that the pricing of such insurance would be better done by the private sector; some of these, (e.g. Chapter 13, by Acharya, Philippon and Richardson in Acharya and Richardson (2009)), have overcome some of the main hurdles to such an exercise. Nevertheless, without wishing to exclude further consideration of such alternative ideas, we shall primarily focus on capital adequacy requirements. In a sense higher capital charges for systemic financial institutions can be seen as a form of public sector insurance premium.

The current Basel II requirements for capital adequacy are pro-cyclical; as ratings migrate downwards in a bust, CARs rise, at a time when profits fall, write-offs increase and capital markets are unwelcoming to additional issues of equity, as evidenced recently (though the value of new capital raised exceeded our initial fears). What had not been sufficiently appreciated beforehand was the extent of interaction between the pro-cyclicality of the CARs and of the emerging mark-to-market, fair value, accounting system, IFRS, especially IFS 39, and FASB, especially FAS 157. That interaction is now well understood and under the US Emergency Economic Act of October 2008, a commission in the USA will study the wider financial implications of using mark-to-market for the financial system, whether its use should be amended, and, if so, how.

We are not in a position to second-guess the outcome of that study, and accounting practices are not our central focus, though we do see problems in moving to any alternative procedure.[13] The point that we do want to emphasize is that the less that can be done to lessen the pro-cyclicality of 'mark-to-market', the more urgent it becomes to put greater weight on switching the effects of macro-prudential regulation from being pro-cyclical to becoming counter-cyclical. We also propose a mark-to-funding framework that (i) reduces procyclicality and (ii) provides incentives to reduce maturity-mismatch. Nevertheless we shall make some further brief comments on this topic in Chapter 5. we shall also deal there, and at rather greater length, with two other current issues, bankers' remuneration and limits on loan to value (and/or loan to income) ratios, plus a few words on other related topics.

A chief criticism of the current system of CARs, Basel I shifting over to Basel II, has been that it appeared to do too little to limit bankers' credit expansion in the boom, nor to help offset the wave of panic, failures and deleveraging in the subsequent crisis. CARs never seemed to bite, and financiers seemed to be able to do as they pleased, aided by much regulatory arbitrage via the shadow banking system and derivative markets, e.g. hedging counter-party risk via CDS.

An effective counter-cyclical macro-prudential policy will be an unpopular policy, since its purpose is to constrain the regulated from doing what they want to do when they want, by legal prohibition or by making it much more expensive. There is a natural incentive to avoid the regulation via a shift of business into the unregulated sector. We describe this as the 'boundary problem', which is described in more detail in Appendix A, largely a reprise of Goodhart (2008). There are two aspects of the boundary problem; the shift of activity to unregulated players; and the use of financial engineering to enable given capital to support more credit. Both are important. In the last boom the use of off-balance-sheet entities was arguably as, or more, serious as the shift to unregulated institutions.

The main point is that the 'boundary problem' is so pervasive that either financial regulation has to be fairly light-touch, so as to avoid massive avoidance via disintermediation, or to be restrictive and prescriptive in the sense of preventing disintermediation via legal prohibition. Our preference is for light-touch regulation, (with one exception on housing loan-to-value ratios, to be discussed later in Chapter 6). In general, restrictive control of financial intermediation stifles inno-

13 Under what circumstances would mark-to-market be suspended and by whose say-so? What alternative would be applied? How would that square with the ideal of transparency?

vation and, especially if government starts to intervene with direct controls over bank lending, interferes with the appropriate allocation of capital.

This poses quite a problem. How do you make regulation counter-cyclical, effective (and hence unpopular), and yet at the same time relatively light touch? This is not easy; indeed if the solution was easy, it would have been discovered and applied long ago. We believe that our proposals, taken as a whole, would help to resolve this dilemma.

There is, indeed, a danger that, in the aftermath of the current crisis, capital requirements will be ratcheted upwards, not only during boom periods, as advocated here, but throughout. That will lower capital returns in banking and other equivalently regulated sectors. The regulated sector would then shrink, relative to unregulated intermediaries and markets, and/or the banks would take on more risk to maintain higher RoEs. Either way intrusive regulation is likely to cause behavioural changes that could usher in the next crisis, in say 20 years time. Regulators, and politicians, simply have to be aware and alert to such an inevitable regulatory dialectic, and try to avoid exacerbating it. That is not so easy, especially when the current turmoil is so acute and fresh in our memory.

A second criticism of the Basel approach to CARs is that they did not do such detailed thinking about incentives and sanctions. Instead, they simply suggested preferred forms of (bank) behaviour. Thus they came out with proposed capital ratios, which then became translated into rigid minima. But such minima became in practice unavailable at times of need. For example banks currently cannot allow their published tier 1 capital to fall below 4%, despite one of the greatest unexpected shocks of all time. In fact, no significant bank would now dare to allow its ratio drop much below about 7-8%, because the market punishes banks even more effectively than supervisors. Far from adding to the resilience of the banking system, such required minima just represent a burden, and may even indeed exacerbate risk-taking by making it harder for bankers to obtain their target return on assets (ROA). Instead what is essential is to devise a calibrated ladder of increasing penalty, as the CAR falls below the 'well capitalised' level; again this largely involves following the lead of the authors of the Federal Deposit Insurance Corporation Improvement Act (FDICIA) of 1991.

2 Nature of Systemic Risk

Before considering the details of future regulation, it is desirable to have a good understanding about the causes of liquidity and solvency problems. If a financial institution is insolvent, it should be closed down (though not necessarily liquidated). However, if the financial problems stem primarily from temporary liquidity problems, then intervention might be justified to save the financial institution. In this Chapter we outline how liquidity problems can lead to solvency problems and how relatively small shocks can cause liquidity suddenly to dry up , carrying the potential for a full-blown financial crisis. We first look at the problems from an individual financial institution's perspective, and then highlight the importance of looking at it from a systemic context. As we outline several amplification mechanisms, it will become apparent that the current philosophy of banking regulation – that you can make the system safe by making individual institutions safe – is an unsatisfactory basis for insuring the stability of the system as a whole.

2.1 Solvency, liquidity and maturity mismatch

A financial institution is insolvent when its 'going concern' value does not exceed the expected value of its liabilities. In normal times, when financial markets are strong, it is fairly easy to identify insolvent financial firms. However, at times of crisis, it is difficult since solvency becomes so co-mingled with liquidity issues. Prices of assets become disconnected from estimates of expected cash flows and, instead, reflect the prices that could be obtained if the assets had to be sold tomorrow to the few investors prepared to buy such assets at such time (the liquidity price).[14]

The mechanisms that explain why liquidity can suddenly evaporate operate through the interaction of funding illiquidity due to maturity mismatches and market illiquidity.

As long as a financial institution's assets pay off whenever its debt is due, it cannot suffer from funding liquidity problems even if it is highly levered. However, financial institutions typically have an asset-liability maturity mismatch and hence are exposed to funding liquidity risk. A funding shortage arises when it is prohibitively expensive both to (i) borrow more funds (low funding liquidity) and

14 Today the divergence is as much as 50% of the asset. Assets where delinquency rates are less than 20%, are trading with an 80% discount to par.

(ii) sell off its assets (low market liquidity). In short, problems only arise if both funding liquidity dries up (high margins/haircuts, restrained lending) and market liquidity evaporates (fire sale discounts).

More specifically, *funding liquidity* describes the ease with which investors and arbitrageurs can obtain funding from financiers. Funding liquidity is high – and markets are said to be 'awash with liquidity' – when it is easy to raise money. Typically, when a leveraged trader, such as a bank, dealer, or hedge fund, purchases an asset, he uses the purchased asset as collateral and borrows (short-term) against it. However, he cannot borrow the entire price. The difference between the security's price and its value as collateral – the margin or haircut – must be financed by the trader's own equity capital. Margin lending is short-term since margins and haircuts can be adapted to market conditions on a daily basis.

Financial institutions that rely substantially on short-term (commercial) paper or repo contracts have to roll over their debt. An inability to roll over this debt-if, for example, the market for commercial paper dries up-is equivalent to margins/haircuts increasing to 100 percent, because the firm becomes unable to use its assets as a basis for raising funds. Similarly, withdrawals of demand deposits or capital redemptions from an investment fund have the same effect as an increase in margins. Funding liquidity risk is due to maturity mismatches and can thus take three forms: 1) margin/haircut funding risk, or the risk that margins and haircuts will change; 2) rollover risk, or the risk that it will be more costly or impossible to roll over short-term borrowing; and 3) redemption risk, or the risk that demand depositors of banks or even equity holders seek to withdraw funds. All three incarnations of funding liquidity risk are only detrimental when assets must be sold only at fire-sale prices-that is, when market liquidity is low.

Market liquidity is low when it is difficult to raise money by selling the asset at reasonable prices. In other words, market liquidity is low when selling the asset depresses the sale price. When market liquidity is low, it is very costly to shrink a firm's balance sheet.

These two liquidity concepts do not exist in a vacuum; they are influenced by the financial soundness of other financial institutions.

Traditionally, capital requirements have been the cornerstone of financial regulation – especially so for banks. The current thinking behind the use of capital requirements is that maintaining a capital buffer allows an institution to absorb losses on its assets and remain solvent, thereby protecting its creditors – notably retail depositors. Moreover, that thinking relies on the reasoning that the solvency of each individual institution ensures the soundness of the financial system as a whole. This thinking leads naturally to the conclusion that the key determinant of the size of the regulatory capital buffer should be some measure of risks associated with the assets of that institution. This is because the degree to which solvency can be ensured depends on the likelihood that the realized value of assets falls below the notional value of the creditors' claim. The original Basel capital accord of 1988 introduced coarse risk buckets into which assets could be classified, but the Basel II rules have taken the idea much further, by refining the gradations of the riskiness of the assets, and fine-tuning the regulatory capital to the risks of the assets held by each bank. Protagonists of Basel II argue that its essential difference with Basel I is that it is far more 'risk-sensitive'.

While this seems reasonable from an individual bank's perspective, it is clear that the level of market and funding liquidity is not exogenously given but determined in the economy as a whole and hence, important adverse feedback effects might arise. This requires a more systemic view of liquidity crises.

2.2 Funding liquidity and the domino model

It is a truism that ensuring the soundness of each individual institution ensures the soundness of the system as a whole. However, for this proposition to be a good prescriptive guide for actions, we need to have confidence that actions that enhance the soundness of a particular institution will invariably promote overall stability. However, the proposition is vulnerable to the fallacy of composition.[15] It is possible, indeed often likely, that attempts by individual institutions to remain solvent can push the system into collapse.

Take a simple example, illustrated by Figure 2. Bank 1 has borrowed from Bank 2. Bank 2 has other assets, as well as its loans to Bank 1. Suppose that Bank 2 suffers credit losses on these other loans, but that the creditworthiness of Bank 1 remains unchanged. The loss suffered by Bank 2 depletes its equity capital. In the face of such a shock, a prudent course of action by Bank 2 is to reduce its overall exposure, so that its asset book is trimmed to a size that can be carried comfortably with the smaller equity capital.

Figure 2 An example of interbank relationships

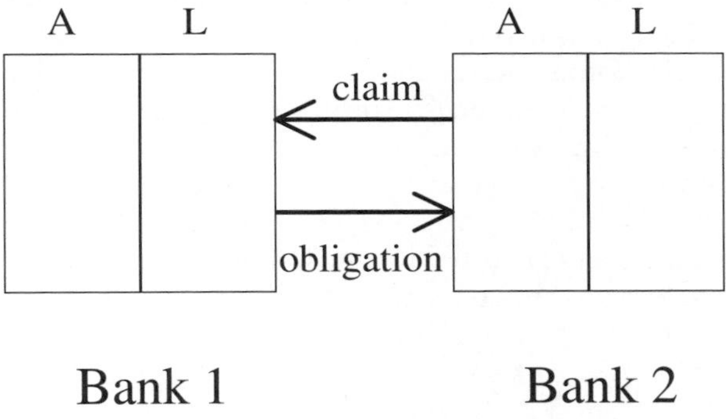

One way to ensure the solvency of Bank 2 is for it to reduce its overall lending, including its lending to Bank 1. By reducing its lending, Bank 2 reduces its risk exposure. However, from Bank 1's perspective, the reduction of lending by Bank 2 is a withdrawal of funding. Unless Bank 1 can find alternative sources of funding, it will have to reduce its own asset holdings, either by curtailing its lending, or by selling marketable assets.

In the case where we have the combination of (i) Bank 1 not having alternative sources of funding, (ii) the reduction in Bank 2's lending being severe, and (iii) Bank 1's assets being so illiquid that they can only be sold at fire sale prices, then

15 See Crockett (2000) "Marrying the Micro- and Macro-Prudential Dimensions of Financial Stability" Bank for International Settlements discussion paper. A fallacy of composition arises when one infers that something is true for the whole from the fact that it is true for each of the individual components of the whole. See Morris and Shin (2008) "Financial Regulation in a System Context" forthcoming in the Brookings Papers on Economic Activity.

Figure 3 The 'domino' model of financial contagion

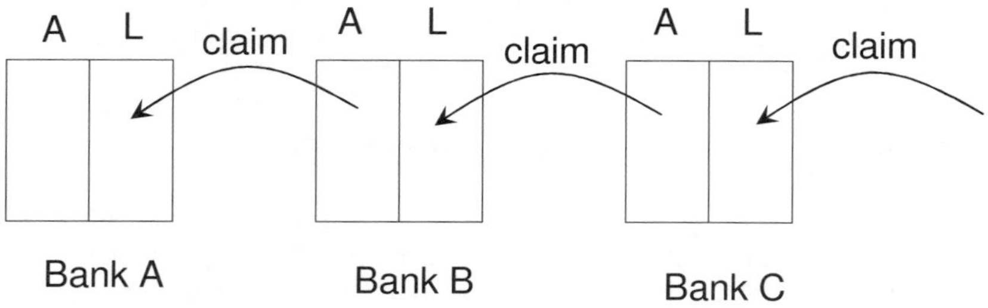

the withdrawal of lending by Bank 2 will feel like a run from the point of view of Bank 1. In other words, a prudent shedding of exposures from the point of view of Bank 2 is a run from the point of view of Bank 1. Arguably, this type of run is what happened to the UK bank Northern Rock, which failed in 2007, as well as the US securities houses Bear Stearns and Lehman Brothers, both of which suffered crippling runs in 2008.

The importance of the liabilities side perspective puts into question the traditional view of how systemic risk propagates throughout the financial system. A naive version of such a view could be depicted in Figure 3.

Here, bank A has borrowed from bank B, and bank B has borrowed from bank C, etc. Then, if A takes a hit and defaults, then bank B will suffer a loss. If the loss is large enough to wipe out B's capital, then B defaults. Bank C then takes a hit. In turn, if the loss is big enough, bank C defaults, etc. We could dub this the 'domino' model of financial contagion.

The domino model of contagion has been examined in numerous simulation studies conducted at central banks, but the universal conclusion has been that the impact of the domino model of contagion is very small. It is only with implausibly large shocks that the simulations generate any meaningful contagion. The reason is that the domino model paints a picture of passive financial institutions who stand by and do nothing as the sequence of defaults unfolds. In practice, however, they will take actions in reaction to unfolding events, and in anticipation of impending defaults.

2.3 Loss spiral – asset price effect

Thus, the domino model does not take sufficient account of how prices and measured risks change, and how such changes impact on the behaviour of market participants. In the simplest scenario of the domino model, asset prices are fixed at their book values, and balance sheets take a hit only with default. Such a view is obsolete in the market-based financial system where balance sheets are marked to market and where financial institutions react to changes in measured risks.

Indeed, defaults need not even be *necessary* to generate contagion. Price changes themselves may be enough. When financial institutions mark their balance sheets to market, changes in prices lead to losses that may be sufficient to transmit the shocks to other institutions even when they do not hold claims against each other. Losses worsen funding liquidity for many financial institutions, forcing them to shed even more assets which further depresses prices and

Figure 4 The loss spiral (balance sheet spiral)

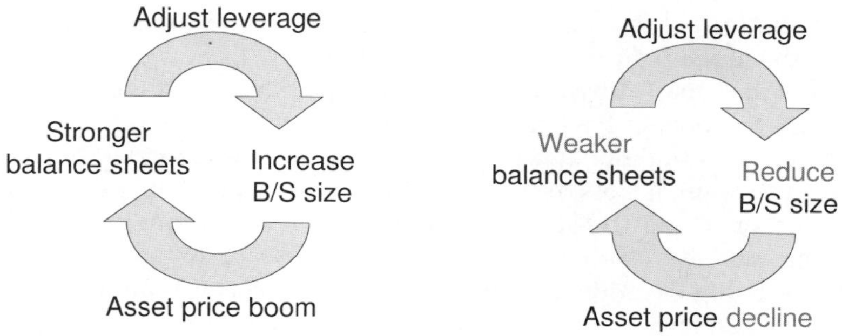

increases losses, and so on. The loss spiral leads to sharp asset price movements especially at times of financial crisis.

If greater demand for the asset puts upward pressure on its price, then there is the potential for a feedback effect in which stronger balance sheets feed greater demand for the asset, which in turn raises the asset's price and lead to stronger balance sheets. Having come full circle, the feedback process goes through another turn. The circular figure on the left in Figure 4 illustrates the feedback during a boom. Note the critical role played by procyclical leverage.

The mechanism works in reverse in downturns. Consider a fall in the price of an asset held widely by hedge funds and banks. Then, the net worth of such an institution falls faster than the rate at which the asset falls in value, eroding its equity cushion. One way that the bank can restore its equity cushion is to sell some of its assets, and use the proceeds to pay down its debt. The circular chart on the right in Figure 4 illustrates the feedback during a bust. Note the importance of marking to market. By synchronizing the actions of market participants, the feedback effects are amplified.

Take the episode of the distress suffered by European life insurance companies in the summer of 2002. By the nature of insurers' balance sheets, they did not borrow from each other as banks do. However, when stock prices plumbed new lows in the summer of 2002, the European life insurers found that their regulatory constraints were beginning to bind. In the U.K., for instance, the usual 'resilience test' applied to life insurance companies in which the firm has to demonstrate solvency in the face of a further 25% stock market decline was beginning to bind. German and Swiss insurers were even more constrained. The remedy for these insurers was to sell stocks, so as to reduce their exposures to them. However, large scale sales merely served to depress prices further, making the constraints bind harder. This generated a further round of selling, and so on. The regulators in the affected countries suspended the solvency tests for several weeks until the crisis abated. For instance, the U.K. Financial Services Authority diluted the resilience test so as to preempt the destabilizing forced sales of stocks by the major market players.[16]

The domino model of contagion is flawed, and is not useful for understanding financial contagion in a modern, market-based financial system. Instead, the key

16 FSA Guidance Note 4 (2002), "Resilience test for insurers". See also FSA Press Release, June 28th 2002, no FSA/PN/071/2002, "FSA introduces new element to life insurers' resilience tests".

to understanding the events of the global liquidity and credit crunch in 2007-08 is to follow the reactions of the financial institutions themselves to price changes, and to shifts in the measured risks.

The transition to a market-based financial system is most advanced in the United States, but its influence has been very profound for the global financial system as a whole. Even for traditional deposit-taking banks, their marginal source of funding has been the capital markets, for example through repurchase agreements or commercial paper. This is because the traditional source of funding such as retail deposits are usually insufficiently flexible to fund expansions of lending. Moreover, the spreading of funding to include capital markets was often seen by banks, regulators and shareholders as increasing the liquidity and hence the solvency of a financial institution To this extent, the traditional distinction between banking and capital markets has become very difficult to draw. Indeed, the leitmotif for the crisis of 2007-8 has been the amplification of the banking crisis through capital market conditions, spurred on by the pervasive use of mark-to-market accounting and market-sensitive risk management systems.

When financial institutions are integrated into the capital markets, market conditions dictate overall funding conditions. The balance sheet dynamics of financial intermediaries that mark their balance sheets to market and use market sensitive risk measures have some distinctive features.

2.4 Margin/haircut spiral

The loss spiral is not purely due to asset price effects, since a leveraged institution that suffers mark-to-market losses of $x has to reduce its position by $x times its leverage ratio.

Figure 5 Two liquidity spirals

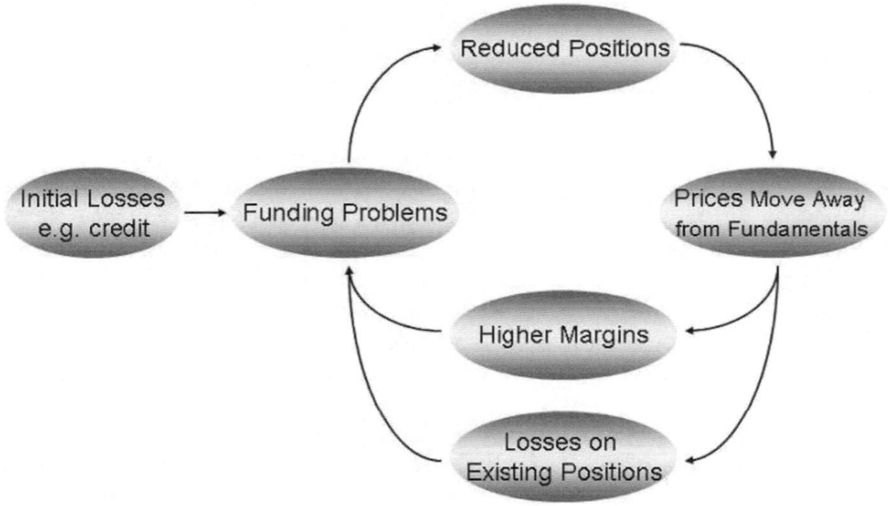

Source: Brunnermeier and Pedersen (2009)

The *margin/haircut spiral* reinforces the loss spiral since it forces the financial institution to reduce its leverage ratio on top of it. Margins and haircuts implicitly determine the maximum leverage a financial institution can adopt. Margins/haircuts spike in times of large price drops and thereby lead to a general tightening of lending. Brunnermeier and Pedersen (2009) – see Figure 5 -- show that a vicious cycle emerges, where higher margins and haircuts force de-leveraging and more sales, which increase margins further and force more sales, leading to the possibility of multiple equilibria. As asset prices drop, risk measures (like Value-at-Risk) increase, which not only lead to higher margins and external funding costs, but also reduce risk-appetite within banks. Risk managers step on the brakes and force traders within a bank to de-lever their positions. Leverage is procyclical. When many market participants de-lever in stressed environments, liquidity disappears down a black hole.[17]

During downturns both spirals force leveraged investors to unwind their positions causing a) more losses and b) higher margins/haircuts and tighter lending standards, which in turn exacerbate the funding problems, and so on. Both spirals lead to procyclicality.

Figure 6 below shows empirical evidence for the margin spiral for the then US investment banks.[18] It shows the scatter chart of the weighted average of the quarterly change in assets against the quarterly change in leverage of the (then) five stand-alone US investment banks – Bear Stearns, Goldman Sachs, Lehman Brothers, Merrill Lynch and Morgan Stanley.

Figure 6 Leverage growth and asset growth of US investment banks

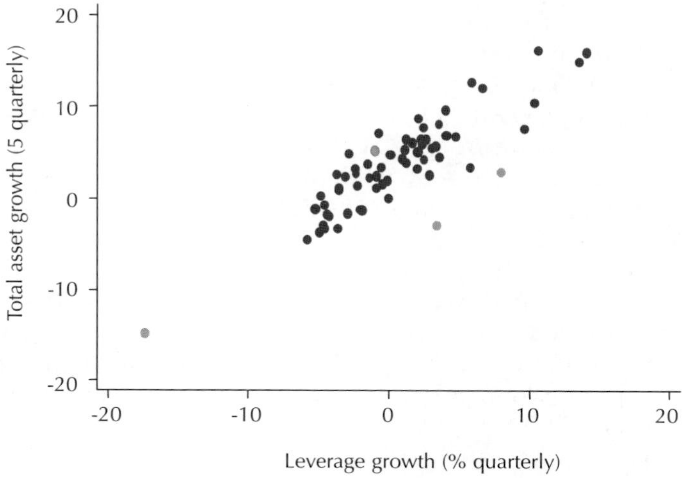

Source: SEC; Adrian and Shin (2007)

17 See Persaud (2002).
18 See Adrian and Shin (2007).

Leverage is high when balance sheets are large, while leverage is low when balance sheets are small. This is exactly the opposite of the traditional finding for households, whose leverage is high when balance sheets are *small*. For instance, if a household owns a house that is financed by a mortgage, leverage falls when the house price increases, since the equity of the household is increasing at a much faster rate than assets[19]. For investment banks, however, the relationship is reversed. It is as if the householder responded to an increase in house prices by increasing the mortgage loan to value ratio so that leverage increases in spite of the increased value of his house.

A procyclical leverage ratio offers a window on the notion of financial system liquidity. When leverage is procyclical, the demand and supply response to asset price changes can amplify shocks. To see this, consider an increase in the price of assets held widely by leveraged market players and intermediaries. The increase in the price of assets strengthens the players' balance sheets, since the net worth of levered players increases as a proportion of their total assets.

When balance sheets become stronger, leverage falls. To the extent that the intermediary wants to avoid holding too much equity (for instance, because return on equity becomes too low), it will attempt to restore leverage. One way it can do so is by borrowing more, and using the proceeds to buy more of the assets it already holds.

There is a more subtle feature of Figure 6 which tells us much about the financing decisions of financial intermediaries. Recall that the horizontal axis measures the (quarterly) change in leverage, as measured by the change in log assets minus the change in log equity. The vertical axis measures the change in log assets. Hence, the 45-degree line indicates the set of points where equity is unchanged. Above the 45-degree line equity is increasing, while below the 45-degree line, equity is decreasing. Any straight line with slope equal to 1 indicates constant growth of equity, with the intercept giving the growth rate of equity.

A feature to note from Figure 6 is that the slope of the scatter chart is close to 1, implying that equity is increasing at a constant rate on average. Thus, equity seems to play the role of the forcing variable, and all the adjustment in leverage takes place through expansions and contractions of the balance sheet rather than through the raising or paying out of equity. Said differently, it shows how the margin spiral and loss spiral reinforce each other.

A closer look at repo haircuts, which determine the implicit maximum leverage that is permitted in collateralized borrowing transactions such as repurchase agreements (repos), is instructive since repos are the primary source of funding for market-based banking institutions. In a repurchase agreement, the borrower sells a security today for a price below the current market price on the understanding that it will buy it back in the future at a pre-agreed price. The difference between the current market price of the security and the price at which it is sold is called the 'haircut' in the repo, and fluctuates together with funding conditions in the market.

The fluctuations in the haircut largely determine the degree of funding avail-

19 This traditional response, may have been eroded by the trend in the most recent boom for home owners to try to benefit from lower interest rates and higher home values by frequent resetting of mortgages.

able to a leveraged institution. The reason is that the haircut determines the maximum permissible leverage achieved by the borrower. If the haircut is 2%, the borrower can borrow 98 dollars for 100 dollars worth of securities pledged. Then, to hold 100 dollars worth of securities, the borrower must come up with 2 dollars of equity. Thus, if the repo haircut is 2%, the maximum permissible leverage (ratio of assets to equity) is 50.

Suppose that the borrower leverages up the maximum permitted level. Such an action would be consistent with the objective of maximizing the return on equity, since leverage magnifies return on equity. The borrower thus has a highly leveraged balance sheet with leverage of 50. If at this time, a shock to the financial system raises the market haircut, then the borrower faces a predicament. Suppose that the haircut rises to 4%. Then, the permitted leverage halves to 25, from 50. The borrower then faces a hard choice. Either it must raise new equity so that its equity doubles from its previous level, or it must sell half its assets, or some combination of both.

Note that the increase in haircuts will do most harm when starting from very low levels. A percentage point increase from 1% to 2% will mean leverage has to fall from 100 to 50. But a percentage point increase from 20% to 21% will have only a marginal effect on the initial leverage of 5. In this sense, the 'chasing of yield' at the peak of the financial cycle is especially precarious, since the unwinding of leverage will be that much more potent.

Times of financial stress are associated with sharply higher haircuts, necessitating substantial reductions in leverage through asset disposals or raising of new equity. The table below is taken from the October 2008 issue of the *Global Financial Stability Report of the International Monetary Fund* (IMF (2008)), and shows the haircuts in secured lending transactions at two dates – in April 2007 before the financial crisis and in August 2008 in the midst of the crisis. Haircuts are substantially higher during the crises than before.

Raising new equity or cutting assets entail adjustments for the borrower. Raising new equity is notoriously difficult in distressed market conditions. But selling assets in a depressed market is not much better. The evidence from the scatter chart in Figure 6 above is that borrowers tend to adjust leverage primarily through adjustments in the size of the balance sheet, leaving equity unchanged, rather than through changes in equity directly.

Table 1 Haircuts on repo agreements (percent)

Securities	April 07	August 08
US treasuries	0.25	3
Investment-grade bonds	0–3	8–12
High-yield bonds	10–15	25–40
Equities	15	20
Senior leveraged loans	10–12	15–20
Mezzanine leveraged loans	18–25	35+
Prime MBS	2–4	10–20
ABS	3–5	50–60

Source: IMF Global Financial Stability Report, October 2008

2.5 Procyclicality and margin spirals

These liquidity spirals are the underlying cause of procyclicality. As asset prices drop, losses mount and margins/haircuts increase.

So far we have not explained why a drop in asset prices leads to higher margins, haircuts and a more cautious attitude towards lending. Should not a lower price reduce the probability of a further decline in the near future? Is not a price reduction that results from a lack of liquidity likely to be temporary, so that investors with the necessary expertise face a great buying opportunity? Hence, one might think that lenders would be willing to lend more freely by lowering margins after prices have dropped. There are at least three reasons why one observes exactly the opposite in the data:

a) Backward-looking risk measures
b) Time-varying volatility
c) Adverse selection.

Margins, haircuts and a bank's internal risk tolerance are typically obtained from risk-measures like Value-at-Risk (VaR). While the definitions of these measures have their own shortcomings, the bigger problem is how they are estimated. Typically these risk measures are estimated naively using past data. Hence, a sharp temporary price drop leads to a sharp increase in the estimates of these risk measures. This hikes margins/haircuts, constrains investors, and may force them to sell off their assets. Paradoxically, the forced fire-sale might, justify the sharp increase in the risk-measure ex-post. For example, as in a boom phase volatility and default estimates are low, margins will be low which allows higher leverage and supports the expansionary phase. When the first adverse shocks hit, the volatility estimates shoot up leading to a deleveraging process described by the margin spiral. In short, if the objective function of individual institutions is to maintain return on equity, or value at risk, leverage will be procyclical. Ideally, one should take such endogenous effects due to risk mismeasurement into account.

Second, the volatility of a price process could be time-varying. A sharp price decline may signal that we are about to enter more volatile times. Consequently, margins and haircuts should be larger and lending should be reduced after such a price decline. An extreme example was the situation in August 2007, when the asset-backed commercial paper market dried up completely. Prior to the crisis, asset-backed commercial paper was almost risk-free because of overcollateralization – i.e. first losses would be assumed by lower tranches. However, in August 2007, the overcollateralization cushion evaporated, making such assets much more risky. Consequently, investors were unwilling to let structured investment vehicles roll-over their debt.

The third reason why margins increase when prices drop is that asymmetric-information frictions emerge. As losses mount, debt becomes more risky and hence more 'information sensitive.' Also, financiers become more careful about whether to accept a pool of assets as collateral since they fear receiving a particularly bad selection of assets. They might, for example, be worried that structured investment vehicles sold the good, 'sellable' assets and left as collateral only the bad, less valuable, 'lemons.'

2.6 Externalities – rationale for regulation

The presence of liquidity spirals per se does not justify government interventions. One must argue from a social welfare perspective that financial institutions over-expose themselves to the risk of getting caught in a liquidity spiral by holding highly levered positions with excessive maturity-mismatches. We argue that this is indeed the case due to the following two risk-spillover externalities that we alluded to in Chapter 1:

a) Fire-sale externalities
b) Interconnectedness externalities

The fire-sale externality arises since each individual financial institution does not take into account the price impact its own fire-sales will have on asset prices in a possible future liquidity crunch. Hence, fire-sales by some institutions spillover, and adversely affect the balance sheet of others, causing a negative externality. This externality is pointed out in Stiglitz (1982) and Geanakoplos and Polemarchakis (1986) and subsequently appeared in numerous academic papers. It is arguably the main rationale for bank regulation.[20]

In general, a financial institution is also not concerned how many others it will drag down, should it fail. Especially the failure of big and interconnected institutions would bring down these negative risk-spillover effects on others. An opaque market structure, as for example in over-the-counter markets (OTC markets), exacerbates these effects.[21]

What makes matters even worse is that the potential prospect of a government bailout gives institutions the incentive to become 'too big to fail' and 'too interconnected to fail.' The larger an institution, or the more interconnected it is, the higher the probability that a financial institution will be bailed out in times of crisis. In short, the current system implicitly subsidizes institutions that cause negative externalities on others. Hence, we will argue in the subsequent Chapter that the regulatory framework has to focus on risk spillovers, i.e., externalities.

In general it might be desirable for the monetary authority to step in after a 'once in a blue moon' liquidity shock[22], since it is socially not optimal for each bank to be required to provision against those shocks. However, since financial institutions expect this, they will alter their behaviour – which provides another rationale for financial regulations.

2.7 Aggregate liquidity expansions and contractions

We conclude this section by recalling that institutions that hold assets with high market liquidity (or short-term assets) can adjust their balance sheet size flexibly by reducing lending and not rolling over debt. However, when the financial sys-

20 While most current risk measures like Value-at-Risk (VaR) focus on the risk of an individual financial institution, Adrian and Brunnermeier (2008) develop a new risk measure, "CoVaR," that explicitly takes the risk spillovers into account.

21 On network effects, see Brunnermeier (2009).

22 Today, this notion has been popularised by Nasim Taleb as a "black swan."

tem as a whole holds long-term, illiquid assets financed by short-term liabilities, any tensions resulting from a sharp, synchronized contraction of balance sheets will show up somewhere in the system. Even if some institutions can adjust down their balance sheets flexibly, there will be pinch points in the system that will be exposed by such de-leveraging.

Fluctuations in leverage in the context of widespread secured lending exposes the myth of 'lump of liquidity' in the financial system. It is tempting to be misled by our use of language into thinking that 'liquidity' refers to a stock of available funding in the financial system which could be redistributed to those who need it most. When liquidity dries up, it disappears altogether rather than being re-allocated elsewhere. When haircuts rise, all balance sheets shrink in unison. Thus, there is a generalized decline in the willingness to lend. When a bank such as Northern Rock finds itself at the receiving end of a run by its creditors, it cannot simply turn to another creditor to take up the slack, for all other creditors are simultaneously curtailing their lending. In this sense, liquidity should be understood in terms of the growth of balance sheets (i.e. as a flow), rather than as a stock.

3 Who Should be Regulated (by Whom)?

In Chapter 2 we provided a theoretical foundations for the regulation of financial firms by outlining an underlying mechanism which leads endogenously to financial instability. The first question one has to address is: Who should be regulated? Since any effective regulation forces firms to deviate from their preferred option, they always have an incentive to move their business outside the boundary of regulation. It is then no surprise that the adverse mechanism described in Chapter 2 reappears in the unregulated sector, which calls then for government support when a crisis hits. Commercial banks setting up associated conduits, SIVs and hedge funds in the last credit bubble is a vivid reminder of this 'boundary problem', which is discussed in further detail in Appendix A.

In this section we propose some guiding principles on the scope of regulation, before emphasizing the importance of counter-cyclical financial regulation (Chapter 4) and liquidity and maturity mismatches (Chapter 5).

3.1 Classification of financial institutions based on objective risk-spillover measures

First, the classification of financial institutions should be based on objective risk measures that capture the risk-spillovers from one institution to the next. This is especially important for macro-prudential regulation. Any financial institution that is subject to systemic risk, not only banks but also other interconnected financial players, like mono-line insurers, insurance companies (like AIG which turn out to be large-scale sellers of credit default-swaps), should be covered by regulation. The fault line of regulation should be primarily determined by the institution's actions and asset-liability structure, while its legal identity as bank, insurance company, SIV etc. should only play a secondary role.

Among others, CoVaR is one such spillover risk measure. For other surveys of systemic risk, see De Bandt and Hartmann (2000) and Ferguson, et al. (2007). CoVaR quantifies how financial difficulties of one institution can increase the tail risk of others.[23] Unlike the typical Value-at-Risk (VaR) measure, which captures the

23 Regressing an index of financial institutions or bank X's counterparties on bank X with quantile regressions is one tractable way to estimate the (non-timevarying) CoVaR. For more details see Adrian and Brunnermeier's working paper titled "CoVaR", *http://www.princeton.edu/~markus/research/papers/CoVaR*. The work by Segoviano, of the IMF, and Goodhart (2009) examining the effect on the Probability of Default of other banks in the system, conditioned on the failure of any specific bank, is another exercise in this same genre.

risk of a single institution, CoVaR captures the links across several institutions. More specifically, bank X's CoVaR is the conditional VaR of bank X's counterparty or the whole financial sector after conditioning that bank X is in difficulty.[24] In particular, if bank X causes some risk spillovers on its counterparties, then the CoVaR exceeds the unconditional VaR. Such a risk spillover measure should be supplemented with stress tests scenarios.

The risk-spillover of a financial player can be high if it (i) *causes* financial difficulties at other institutions or it is (ii) *simply correlated* with financial difficulties amongst other financial institutions. A good risk-spillover measure should encompass both channels, but this distinctions helps us to group financial institutions as:

1. 'Individually systemic'
These institutions cause risk spillovers and include institutions that are so large, so massively interconnected, and so iconic as `national champions' that no government would ever allow them to fail. They require macro-prudential regulation and also micro-prudential regulation (e.g. Solvency II) due to their size.

2. 'Systemic as part of a herd' (e.g., highly levered hedge funds)
These may be sufficiently small, and insignificant, for their *individual* condition not to be of great concern to the authorities, particularly when this is driven primarily by idiosyncratic factors, but when they move together as part of a larger group, their correlated fluctuations may well be systemic. Hence, they require some macro-prudential regulation but very limited micro-prudential regulation which might, in the case of hedge funds, be executed via their prime-brokers.[25]

3. Non-systemic large and not highly levered (e.g., Insurance Companies and Pension funds)
These institutions need full micro-prudential regulation, but no additional macro-prudential regulation.

4. Tinies, especially if they are unlevered, should have minimal conduct of business regulations.

The risk-spillover measure should determine whether a firm needs macro-prudential regulation (group 1 and 2) or not (group 3 and 4) and influence the extent of the capital and liquidity charges. For example, an insurance company like AIG that sells credit default swaps (CDS) on a large scale belongs to group 1 instead of 3.

Each year, and on the occasion of each major market event, the relevant regulators and supervisors should, as a matter of course, draw up a list of which financial institutions they consider to be 'systemic', and share such information with other supervisors.

---

24 The same "conditioning-method" can be used for any risk-measure and is not restricted to VaR, which is not the ideal risk measure. The "co-expected shortfall" is an alternative spillover risk measure.

25 Madoff's fund did not use a separate prime broker, since he had his own broker/dealer business. This was akin to allowing front and back offices to merge, and should never have been allowed.

At one stage we proposed that the regulators/supervisors should publish that list, in order to enhance the discipline that would impose on regulators/supervisors to do this exercise carefully. But we have been persuaded that the disadvantages of that course outweigh the advantages. Not only is the concept of 'systemic' fuzzy and state-contingent, but also it could lead to moral hazard and to artificial behaviour among the regulated in their attempt to achieve their desired status; this may represent a case for 'constructive ambiguity'.[26]

3.2 Rules for individually systemic institutions

Let us revert to institutions that are individually systemic. There should be serious concern about allowing *any* of them individually to get into trouble. That means that micro-prudential regulation and supervision remain relevant. The established form of such micro-prudential regulation for banks remains Basel II. We advocate that this continues to be applied, as originally proposed, to large systemic, international banks, and that the appropriate micro-prudential controls continue also to be applied to large unlevered institutions.

This is not to say that the methods for assessing risk-weighted assets (RWAs) do not need reform; they do. As has been exemplified throughout the current financial crisis, the risks to a bank's liquidity and capital arise in large part from that bank's off-balance-sheet exposures and contingent liabilities, e.g., in back-up lines of credit to connected conduits, SPVs, SIVs, etc., and in derivative markets. The Basel Committee has done good work, which needs to be extended further now, in assessing how such contingent commitments should be incorporated into measures of RWAs.

Moreover, credit ratings, whether by CRAs or by the banks themselves, are a measure of expected loss, not of unexpected loss. For the latter, what one needs is some estimate of the likelihood of downwards rating migration, and of the resulting scale of loss in that event: a difficult exercise, but not impossible.[27]

More attention should also be given to diversification, but care should be given to distinguishing between idiosyncratic and systemic diversification.[28] A bank which concentrates, for example, totally on loans to a particular category of borrowers in a particular region has no idiosyncratic diversification; i.e., it is subject to certain obvious risks, (i.e. if demand for such borrowers' products declines). However, being unlike most other banks, it is less likely to cause contagion, or spill-over risks, should it fail. Such a bank is, therefore, less dangerous to the system as a whole, and needs no particular extra macro-prudential regulation. It can make its own choices, without external pressure. Idiosyncratic concentration does not cause systemic spill-over risk.

Rules should also be designed in such a way that banks have no incentive to move assets into off-balance sheets vehicles and conduits. As outlined in Brunnermeier (2009) under the current system banks had an incentive to park and

26 One possible way to increase the discipline on the regulators/supervisors would be for them to disclose and discuss their list in a closed session before a Select Committee of their Legislature once every year.

27 The maturity adjustment in the IRB approach of Basel II can be seen as a rough attempt to take into account the possibility of downwards rating migration.

28 On this topic, recent papers by Acharya and Yorulmazer, and by W. Wagner are germane.

diversify assets in off-balance sheet vehicles in order to maintain a lower capital charge.

3.3 Rules for institutions that are 'systemic in a herd'

We now consider the larger number of smaller institutions, mostly small banks, foreign branches and subsidiaries, most hedge funds, private equity, etc., who are not individually systemic, but may become so when they move together as a group (or herd). Consider a system of *n* different banks, where each has a portfolio consisting of an identical fraction ($1/n$) of the aggregate portfolio, (a representative bank system in effect). If one bank fails, the likelihood is that all will. A risk-spillover measure would calculate the aggregate bank portfolio in the country, and then compute how much the individual banks' portfolios correlate with the aggregate. The higher such correlation, the less diversified the system. As usual with risk assessment, co-variance is more important than variance. Since we focus on (left) tail-events, co-risk measures are superior to simple covariance measures.

The problem with Basel II was not so much that it was an incorrect metric of micro-prudential risk (though, of course, it was to some extent), but that it took insufficient account of macro-prudential risk, as set out and argued in Chapter 2. We argue that better measures of macro-prudential risk are to be found in leverage ratios, maturity mismatches and estimates of bank credit expansion and asset price expansions.

This group is currently divided in its view how to regulate this group of financial institutions for micro-prudential purposes. One view is that this wider range of (individually non-systemic) intermediaries should still be subject to individual micro-prudential regulation. Controlling their individual assumption of risk remains, on this view, both a desirable and appropriate function of regulation/supervision. If such micro-prudential supervision is in force, then the macro-prudential factors can be interacted with them along exactly the same lines, as we propose in the following Chapters for systemic institutions.

The other view is that, if an institution is not itself 'systemic', there are no theoretical grounds for external interference in its own chosen risk profile; so, on this view, there would be no need for *any* micro-prudential regulation. Instead, all that would be required would be some simplified macro-prudential requirements, relating core capital to leverage and, perhaps, the intermediary's rate of asset expansion (growth).

Perhaps each country's regulators/supervisors could choose between these alternatives, which could also differ between types of intermediaries, thus banks could be treated differently from hedge funds.

3.4. International considerations for international entities

Typically one of the greatest concerns amongst both banks and politicians relates not so much to competitive inequalities amongst and between domestic banks, but those between domestic owned banks and subsidiaries and branches of foreign banks. Our principle is that the country or entity that bears the burden in case of a bailout of a financial institution should also be in charge of regulating that financial institution. Hence, we would suggest that any branch (of foreign-owned) banks designated as 'systemic' by a host country should automatically be required to change its status to being a separately capitalised subsidiary. Then exactly the same capital and liquidity adequacy requirement calculations would apply to foreign-owned *systemic* subsidiaries[29] as to domestic banks .

As a consequence, if a bank should choose to open branches/subsidiaries in a foreign country that are large enough to be defined by that host country as 'systemic', then it will have to hold a separate pot of capital in that country, according to the host country's calculations. That will reduce the synergies of cross-border banking. It also raises the question of whether (and how far) such separate pots should/could go to satisfy the CAR of the consolidated bank. Our view is that regulators/supervisors are primarily concerned about conditions in their own countries (as has certainly appeared to be the case in practice in the current crisis). If so, the home regulator would relate the CAR to the RWA/Leverage ratio in the home country plus the 'non-systemic' branches/subsidiaries in other countries. We realise that this would be unpicking a part of the prior principle of consolidation on the home regulator.

We would encourage a more European approach within the Euro area. If burden sharing could be agreed upon within Euroland, regulation could be transferred to a European institution.

29 If a subsidiary, or a branch, of a foreign-owned bank sited in some country, (especially in an off-shore centre), was primarily engaged in foreign-currency, entrepot, business, (e.g. intermediating in euro-markets), we would assume that the host country would not categorize that subsidiary/branch as being 'systemic' in its own market. Perhaps foreign-owned banks might want to divide their operations in a host country into two parts, a non-systemic branch running f.c. entrepot operations, and a, possibly systemic, subsidiary dealing mainly in host country business.

4 Counter-Cyclical Regulation

In Chapters 1 and 2, we noted the pro-cyclicality that follows from banks chasing returns on equity, maintaining value at risk, and using mark-to-market valuation and risk approaches. We also highlighted the substantial risks for the financial and economic system when the cycle turns down. In this Chapter and the next, we describe how counter-cyclical regulation may be put in place. There are two main strands of financial regulation, one on capital and one on liquidity. We discuss capital regulation in this section and new approaches to the regulation of liquidity in Chapter 5. The main principles that we invoke are:

1. The main objective of counter-cyclical regulation should be to reduce the systemic risk that fluctuations in the conditions of an institution, or market, would have on the rest of the system. Systemic institutions (markets) should be regulated in direct proportion to their systemic risk. To achieve this, CARs are needed that are based on better risk spillover measures that take leverage, maturity mismatch and financing into account.
2. The measures have to be counter-cyclical, i.e. tough during a credit boom and more relaxed during a crisis. We propose a laddered response to ensure a prompt resolution of emerging problems before they can spill over to the wider financial system.
3. To ensure strict adherence and implementation of such rules, it is important to put an incentive structure for regulators in place and guarantee their independence from political and lobbying pressure.

4.1 Focus on systemic risk spillovers

Capital charges should focus on the risk spillovers an institution causes, or is correlated with, rather than simply the institution's individual risk. As noted earlier, current required minimum capital adequacy ratios provide very little resilience and support to the system. Even so, we still advocate a low, fixed minimum leverage ratio for capital, not as a protection for the regulated banks, but as a protection for the deposit insurance fund (DIF) and the taxpayer, and as a trigger for prompt corrective action. This could be set as a low percentage of total balance-sheet assets and a low liquidity risk measure (as outlined in Chapter 5). Since the objective here is a simple protection for the DIF, a leverage ratio would seem more appropriate than a RWA basis, but we are not fixed on this view. Under FDICIA (1991) this percentage was set as 2%, though the arguments for choosing this rather than another number are not clear (at least to us). Overall, however, the focus should be on risk spillovers that potentially undermine the financial system as a whole.

4.2 When to look out for systemic risk?

Most financial crises are preceded by asset price bubbles. Bubbles often emerge after financial liberalizations or innovations and can persist since even rational sophisticated investors find it more profitable to ride a bubble rather than to go against it. This is in sharp contrast to efficient market hypothesis, but supported by empirical findings.[30] Herding behaviour among financial institutions which are evaluated against the same benchmark are further contributing factors.

Counter-cyclical regulation should be most constraining during the height of a bubble. In the past, regulation followed a 'benign neglect' policy with respect to bubbles. One justification for this approach was the argument that bubbles are difficult to identify with certainty. We find this reasoning unconvincing, since such an argument could be brought forward for almost any important policy decision. We favour a 'lean against the wind' risk-management approach. We argue that such a leaning should be primarily done by counter-cyclical regulatory measures, such as we propose here, not solely via interest rates.[31] Financial authorities should be alerted when clear indications of a bubble emerge, even if the bubble cannot be identified for certain.

The regulation should be particularly effective for bubbles whose bursting might adversely affect the financial intermediation sector. While the bursting of the technology bubble in the early 2000s caused a lot of localised disruption, it bears no comparison to the turmoil which the bursting of the credit and housing bubble has caused. The big difference between them was that the technology bubble did not severely damage the lending sector. Said differently, it is important to determine whether a current funding and credit expansion is sustainable or subject to sudden reversals, with detrimental consequences for the economy. While monetary policy can have some role in 'leaning against the wind' approach, bank regulation is central in controlling excesses in lending practices.

4.3 Predicting institutions' future systemic risk contributions

The problem with Basel II was not so much that it was an incorrect metric of micro-prudential risk (though, of course, it was also that to some extent)[32], but

30 Abreu and Brunnermeier (2003) provide theoretical reasoning why rational traders prefer to ride the bubble rather attack against it. Brunnermeier and Nagel (2004) provide empirical support for this finding.

31 We continue to support the adoption and maintenance of inflation targets, and interest rate policy is primarily predicated to the achievement of such targets.

32 'In particular, the risk weighting applied to mortgage lending was far too low to maintain bank solvency in the event of a severe downturn in the housing market. Not only was there particular pressure to keep this weighting low, but also the regulators may have been infected by the same over-optimism about future housing prices as were the Credit Rating Agencies..

that it took insufficient account of macro-prudential and systemic risk, as set out and argued in Chapter 2. Better measures of macro-prudential risk are to be found. One such measure is CoVaR. However, many risk measures suffer from the shortcoming that they may be procyclical if naively applied, meaning that the application relies on past data when the circumstances and motivations of the actors were different. After a boom phase estimated volatility and correlations are low, and a subsequent price drop would lead to a drastic jump in such estimated risk measures. This would trigger a procyclical margin spiral as described in Chapter 2. Hence, we propose that charges should not be directly based on the current values of systemic risk measures like CoVaR, but rather on variables that predict future CoVaR values. Such variables include leverage, maturity mismatch, interconnectedness measures and estimates of bank credit expansion. This method of relying on more frequently observed variables that predict future CoVaR measures not only allows for countercyclical regulation, but also helps to determine how much weight one should put on each of these variables. Overall, the basic premise is that institutions that cause more negative externalities (risk spillovers) should face higher charges and using predictive analysis ensures a countercyclical regulation.

4.4 How to impose charges

To internalise these systemic externalities, regulators have the choice between the following four forms of charges.

(i) Capital Charge (which impose a cap on the debt/equity ratio)
(ii) Pigovian Tax (which charge a periodic fee from financial institutions)
(iii) Private insurance scheme
(iv) Public/private insurance scheme

The current Basel regulation imposes capital charges in the form of caps on the risk-weighted assets to equity ratio. We see this approach as the one with the least policy obstacles and hence focus our report on it. Nevertheless, one should mention that cap-limits can stifle competition. An explicit Pigovian tax does not have this disadvantage. In addition, it is a more salient policy tool since it affects directly the profit of financial institutions and enters into the income statement. We find a private insurance scheme less attractive for two reasons: First, the government is a natural insurance provider since it is easier for the government to raise funds in times of crisis due to the generalised flight to quality. Second, the recent experience with mono-line insurers has exposed the connection between credit risk and counterparty risk. We have doubts that private insurance schemes can be fully effective in times of severe crisis. Finally, the joint public/private insurance scheme has the advantage that it relies on a private price discovery process and is similar in spirit to many demand deposit insurance scheme (for instance in Germany). While we recognise its advantages, it is not clear to us that markets have a long enough horizon nor the aligned incentives to arrive at the optimal counter-cyclical charges.

Since we foresee huge political economy obstacles for any other way than the capital charge approach, we advocate sticking to it as the basic template, but combining the RWAs (Basel II) approach with measures of maturity mismatch, market and funding liquidity and other variables that predict future systemic risk exposure. Having several measures has the advantage that the regulation is less subject to gaming.

More specifically, we propose multiplying the basic CAR, estimated under Basel II, by a factor, or factors, relating to macro-prudential/systemic risk.

We have to determine two elements:

(i) the factor and how to compute it
(ii) which capital ratio (tier 1 or tier 2) to multiply.

With respect to computing the macro-prudential factor, quantitative impact studies complemented by detailed hypothetical theoretical modeling exercises should determine the linkage to co-risk measures and the weights on maturity mismatch, credit and asset price expansion;[33] and also the time periods over which such expansion should be estimated, though always needing to remember that regulation will change prior behaviour. Highly levered and fast growing 'systemic' institutions would be subject to higher capital requirements than the rest, since they would be more likely to impose spill-over effects on the rest of the system. The idea is that when there is increasing systemic risk, with increasing leverage, maturity mismatch, credit expansion and asset price increases, the multiplication factor would be greater than unity, while it is less than unity during periods of deleveraging.

With respect to the relevant *capital ratio*, one problem is that there are several Basel II ratios, notably the core Tier 1 ratio, the 4% Tier 1 ratio and the 8% Tier 1 plus Tier 2 ratio. In the 1980s, largely in the context of the Basel Committee on Banking Supervision (BCBS) deliberations on the Basel I Capital Accord, there were extensive and robust discussions on the definition of capital. Few since then, have had any enthusiasm or stomach for re-opening this issue. Nevertheless if our intention is to interact a Basel II CAR with macro-prudential, counter-cyclical factors, we have to choose (or to propose) what should be the relevant ratio for doing so. It is our view that, as the recent crisis has progressed, the market has come to place most weight on the core Tier 1 ratio, and, for reasons already set out in Chapter 2, we tend to concur with that. So we would propose interacting macro-prudential factors with the core Tier 1 ratio for each bank (and/or systemic bank subsidiary). But the choice of *micro-prudential ratio* for inter-active purposes is not a matter on which our group has strong views. Our focus is on core tier 1 capital and the systemic risk factor that determines how large it should be. We do not have strong views on how the other (lower) capital tiers should be adjusted when there is an adjustment in the systemic risk factor for core tier 1 capital, but one natural candidate would be that all other capital levels should be go up by the same absolute amount. That is, when the core tier 1 capital goes up by one dollar, all lower tier capital levels should go up by one dollar, also.

---

33 There have been other suggestions as well. John Williamson (private correspondence) would advocate using a measure of departure from estimated equilibrium values, and Repullo, et al., (2009), would propose using nominal GDP growth rates.

4.5 More on bank capital: two notions

In the discussion of which Basel II ratio to interact with our macro-prudential, counter-cyclical, controls, it may help to draw a conceptual distinction between two notions of bank capital. There is, first, the notion of bank capital (implicit in the Basel approach) as a buffer against loss that protects depositors. Under this first notion of bank capital, hybrid claims such as preferred equity or subordinated debt are counted as bank capital, since both are claims that are junior to depositors. Indeed, under the Basel capital accord, subordinated debt counts as Tier 2 capital.

However, there is a second, contrasting notion of bank capital as the claim held by the owners of the bank who have control over the bank's operations.

Arguably, hybrid claims such as preferred shares or subordinated debt do not qualify as bank capital under this second notion of bank capital, as they can be seen as junior forms of debt. When the bank has too little capital in this second sense, the owners' incentives reflect their highly leveraged balance sheet. When faced with a dwindling stake in a leveraged entity, the owners with control have little to lose, and everything to gain by engaging in risk-shifting bets on the bank. The increased repo haircut imposed by the capital market during distress episodes could be seen as the increased margin demanded by creditors in the capital market to changed circumstances.

The key point is that the repo haircut and the implied maximum leverage is a constraint imposed by the capital market, and reflects the terms on which creditors are willing to lend to those with control over the leveraged entity. One plausible channel through which the constraint operates is the wish by creditors to avoid being embroiled in a lengthy and costly bankruptcy settlement after the borrower has defaulted. When a bank breaches the maximum leverage ratio permitted by the market, the bank must take remedial action to reduce its leverage, or face a run by its creditors.

Northern Rock's demise illustrates these issues starkly. Northern Rock was a highly leveraged institution when considering the leverage on common equity. Its high leverage made it especially vulnerable to a deterioration in overall funding conditions for the financial system as a whole.

Figure 7 plots the leverage of Northern Rock from June 1998 to December 2007, using three different measures of equity. Common equity is the most basic form of equity – it is the stake held by the owners of the bank with voting power and hence who have the right to exercise control over the bank. 'Shareholder equity' in Figure 7 is defined as common equity plus preferred shares. Finally, 'total equity' in Figure 7 is shareholder equity plus subordinated debt, a class of debt that is senior to the common and preferred equity, but which is junior to other types of debt taken on by the bank, including deposits.

Figure 7 shows very explicitly how important it is to calculate the leverage ratio with common equity in the denominator. Leverage based on total equity creates the false impression that Northern Rock might have no difficulty rolling over its short-term funding.

Figure 7 Northern Rock's leverage, June 1998 – December 2007

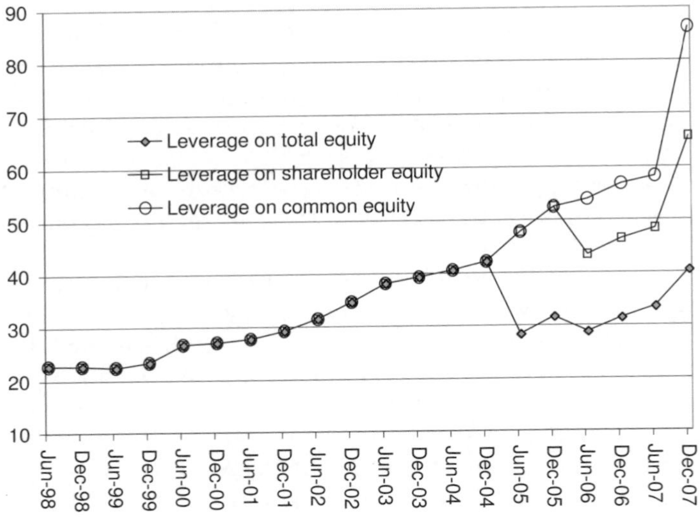

Source: Shin (2008).

4.6 Ladder of responses

With regards to the second main principle, that regulation should be most constraining during credit booms, we propose a propose a prompt and laddered response when a financial institution violates our much more stringent capital and liquidity requirements starting at an earlier stage. We follow the successful implementation of a laddered approach introduced by the FDICIA. For example, when the capital and liquidity requirements are, say 1% below target value, supervision could be enhanced. When the target is missed by 2%, the institution could in addition be forbidden to pay out dividends or make other forms of equity payouts. A missed target by 3% might disallow any bonus payments to the CEO and other board members. A miss by 4 % could require recapitalization or closure within two months.

4.7 Forced debt-equity conversion

Recapitalisation of banks in times of crisis is often difficult because banks suffer from a debt-overhang problem. New investors are unwilling to inject new equity, since the primary beneficiaries of it would be existing debt holders and not the bank itself. To overcome this problem, we propose that the regulators have the authority to convert such existing debt as counts as tier 1 and tier 2 capital into equity. The aim of this tool is alleviate a systemic crisis and, hence, it should only be invoked when the whole or part of the financial sector is in difficulty.

4.8 Clear incentives for regulators: rules versus discretion

The third main principle that we propose is that objective criteria and pre-specified rules should be put forward to guarantee that financial regulation is strictly enforced. To ensure that the enforcement of these rules is credible, regulators must face the right incentive structure[34] and enjoy a degree of independence that allows them to impose potentially unpopular steps. When everyone is calling for more regulation, e.g., as now, just after a crisis, it is not needed at all, since bank managers are timid and risk averse. When regulation *is needed*, no one wants it, because asset prices are rising, there is a boom, everyone is optimistic, and regulation just gets in the way (see Appendix A). Almost every regulator/supervisor will seek maximum discretion. Because of the above considerations, regulation should be based on pre-set rules; otherwise, few regulator/supervisors will actually dare to face the odium of tightening in boom conditions. There is actually little that we are proposing here that in principle and in theory could not have been accomplished under the discretionary Pillar 2 of Basel II. In practice it was not used that way at all, and probably never would be.

4.9 Cross-country considerations

Countercyclical measures should be applied on a country-by-country basis, since cycles are not identical and matching across all parts of the world. Thus Germany and Italy did not share in the housing cycle that affected USA, UK, Spain, etc. Credit expansion took place at a very different pace in various countries. So we cannot, and should not, as yet talk about a world cycle. However, for certain regions, notably the euro-area, countries could coordinate countercyclical measures on a wider regional basis. Thus, even though the Basel II basic CARs are level across countries, the actual interacted counter-cyclical CARs would become higher in countries with an asset boom and rapid credit expansion, than in countries not exhibiting such conditions.

4.10 Contrast to Spanish dynamic provision mechanism

It may be worthwhile comparing and contrasting our approach with that of the Spanish pre- (or dynamic) provisioning mechanism.[35] They are closely similar in intent and construction. Both use macro-prudential measures to interact with prudential requirements. We put more weight on leverage ratios and maturity mismatch;[36] the Spanish put more weight on credit growth (compared to longer-term average values); both would apply numerical coefficients, which have been pre-set, to adjust prudential requirements to the relevant individual banks, including

34 Perhaps with salaries (and pensions) for senior officials inversely related to the measured probability of default of the largest five banks in the country?

35 On the Spanish procedures, see Jimenez and Saurina (2006) and de Lis, et al, (2000).

36 The danger of leverage is greater, the worse the mismatch between funding and asset maturities. The weight to be placed on leverage ratios in macro-prudential CARs should vary inversely with the degree to which our proposals on Liquidity (Chapter 5) are adopted.

subsidiaries of foreign banks in Spain. The Spanish scheme relates solely to credit growth and provisions in Spain. Just as in the case of our proposals, if the Spanish scheme were applied more widely to other countries, its application would differ from country to country depending on the state of the cycle in each country.

A complication of the Spanish pre-provisioning scheme is that it appears to run foul of the accountants and of IFRS (and the tax authorities?). A disadvantage of our proposal is that, by interacting (national) macro-prudential factors with the Basel II CAR, it ends the single level-playing-field for cross-border capital requirements and, with that, the simplicity of head-quarter management and of overall consolidation/control by the home regulator/supervisor. Under our proposal here much more control would flow back to each (systemic) subsidiary and to its host regulator.

While we applaud the principles of Spanish pre-provisioning, we do not think that its quantitative effect has been to moderate the credit cycle by as much as our mechanism could. Nevertheless should the proposal outlined here be regarded as too radical, the universal adoption of the Spanish pre-provisioning scheme (and the adjustment of IFRS to allow that to occur) would represent 'counter-cyclical-lite.'

4.11 Conclusion

The need is to achieve counter-cyclical regulatory mechanism(s). Details of how this might be achieved are important, but secondary. Some practitioners have found our inter-active proposals complex, and doubt whether these could be made operational. If more effective alternatives could be obtained, we would be happy. As Chairman Deng said, 'The colour of the cat is unimportant, so long as it can catch mice.'

5 Regulation of Liquidity and Maturity Mismatches

We have argued in previous Sections that the current philosophy of banking regulation – that you can make the system safe[37] by making individual institutions safe – is an unsatisfactory basis for insuring systemic stability. One of the principal reasons for regulating banks, over and above the way we regulate other businesses, is that their inter-relationships are such that the rational response of one prudent institution to an unexpected loss – a reduction in lending and a sale of assets – may have systemic implications for other prudent institutions. These systemic implications are compounded by herding behaviour and the use of contemporaneous prices in measures of asset value and risk, as discussed in Chapter 3.[38]

In Chapter 2 we indicated that, while traditional views of systemic risk are based on contagious bank failure, a key avenue through which systemic risk flows today is via funding liquidity combined with adverse asset price movements due to low market liquidity.[39] For example, it is worth reiterating that in the case of Northern Rock, Lehman Brothers and Bear Stearns, the failure was precipitated by the inability of these firms (i) to roll over their liabilities (funding illiquidity) and (ii) to sell mortgage products at non-fire sale-prices (market illiquidity), rather than their finding that their borrowers did not pay up (credit risk). Moreover, the freezing of the interbank market, the asset backed commercial paper market, and other sources of funding was more systemic than specific to certain institutions.

This chapter seeks to develop a regulatory approach to liquidity that may make systemic liquidity events less frequent or severe. More specifically, we propose the following two measures:

Mark-to-funding accounting rule

Pools of assets for which long-term funding is secured can be put in a 'hold-to-funding account' linked to the maturity of the funding and do not have to be marked-to-market. We believe this will help to reduce the market illiquidity caused by a forced sale of assets that has no other motivation than the value accounting standard.

37 For a more detailed explanation of this assessment of the current approach to regulation see Nugee and Persaud (2006).
38 See Persaud (2000).
39 See Brunnermeier and Pedersen (2009).

Explicit capital charge for liquidity risk
Financial institutions who hold assets with low market liquidity and long-maturity and fund them with short-maturity assets should incur a higher capital charge. We believe this will internalise the systemic risks these mis-matches cause and incentive banks to reduce funding liquidity risk. Special emphasis should be given to the systemic component, e.g. to the fact that market liquidity at times of crisis is low.

Before explaining the specifics of these two separate but related proposals, we outline why it is inadequate solely to consider the payoff quality of assets and essential to consider liquidity aspects.

5.1 Focusing solely on assets' expected payoffs is insufficient

We argue that focusing exclusively on the quality of a bank's asset portfolio is insufficient, even though the bank's asset quality and its ability to access funding liquidity are related. Historically, bank supervisors hoped that this relationship would be strong enough to make capital adequacy requirements sufficient for dealing with the issue of liquidity.[40] If there had been little doubt about the quality of assets, a liquidity crisis might not have emerged. However, it seems also likely that the crisis would have been more modest in the first instance and potentially more containable if the same assets had been funded with longer-term liabilities. Assets would not have been sold in distressed fashion in such an environment, prices might not then have collapsed so far and the feedback cycle of prices and risk might have been weaker.

5.2 Funding liquidity and maturity mismatch

The financial system's reliance on short-term funding of long-term assets with potentially low market liquidity has been the main source of instability in this and previous financial crises. One of the most critical lessons of this crisis is that, while regulators have been focused on asset quality, systemic risk has as much to do with how assets are funded.[41] If two institutions have the same asset, but one funds with long-term debt and the other by borrowing overnight from the money markets, there is a a substantial difference to the potential for systemic risk. Yet current regulatory rules make little distinction between how the same assets are funded. The absence of distinction gives banks an incentive to fund assets short-term. This incentive is most pronounced when the yield curve is upward sloping, as is often

40 In the first meeting of the Basle Committee of Bank Supervisors (BCBS) in February 1975, the Chairman George Blunden, said '- the Committee's main objective was to help ensure bank solvency and liquidity'. "From the outset, the BCBS appreciated that solvency and liquidity were interrelated; both were essential for the stability and survival of a banking system. An illiquid bank (system) would not remain solvent for long, nor an insolvent bank (system) remain liquid", C. A. E. Goodhart, in a forthcoming volume on the early history of the Basel Committee on Banking Supervision

41 Much of this argument was foreshadowed in Rohner and Shepheard-Walwyn (2000), especially the passage in Section 4 on 'The interaction between capital and liquidity management'.

the case in a boom, and short-term funding is cheaper than long-term funding. There was a collective reliance on short-term, wholesale market funds in the run-up to the 2007 crash.[42]

Is maturity mismatch an inevitable feature of a private banking system? After all, is not banking all about borrowing short and lending long? Not necessarily. There are many caveats to that generalization, and it is also a matter of degree. Small business will complain that, given the onerous covenants on bank loans, they do not feel that they have borrowed long-term from banks. And it is often said that depositors are more likely to have divorced their spouse than leave their bank. Retail demand deposits are not as instant as they appear[43]. The ever-declining ratio of private sector domestic deposits to total liabilities, as banks increasingly relied on short-term wholesale deposits in the run up to the crash of 2007, was one measure of increasing funding liquidity risk amongst banks. Effectively, banks' maturity mismatch got worse through wholesale financing.

5.3 Mark-to-funding – a new accounting rule

We propose a new accounting rule in order (i) to reduce, in an manner that is true to the economic situation of the firm, the procyclicality which mark-to-market induces in asset booms and bust due to the 'loss spiral'. We are as much concerned about the over-expansion in booms as by the crashes in busts; indeed the former often causes the latter. However, we are particularly worried that price declines in a crash force institutions with medium-term funding or liabilities to sell them in order to comply with prudential risk rule fed off mark-to-market valuations, leading to further price declines that in turn force further sales. We are also concerned that concern over mark-to-market volatility keeps buyers at bay in a crisis even when assets are seen to be 'cheap'. Mark-to-market volatility is highlighted as the main reason why credit investors are not buyers of instruments today that have been heavily marked down in price. Moreover, it seems to us that where assets are backed with long-term funding, applying and responding to mark-to-market value accounting, quite apart from the systemic implications described above, is not in the prudential interests of the firm.

We are uncomfortable with any attempt to move accounting valuations away from a fair reflection of the real conditions facing a firm.[44] Indeed, we feel one of the few things worse than mark-to-market accounting is allowing it in the booms and suspending it in periods of market decline, or for assets to be simply shifted from the available-for-sale and trading books onto the hold-to-maturity (banking) book, where they can be valued differently, but where the bank's have no real

---

42 Much of this argument was foreshadowed in Rohner and Shepheard-Walwyn (2000), especially the passage in Section 4 on 'The interaction between capital and liquidity management'.

43 An added systemic risk in the UK case was that a significant amount of wholesale funding was external to the UK. When the crisis hit, there was a 'sudden stop' and littel return of this source of funding.

44 Although financial stability concerns are now paramount, when we get out of the crisis investor protection concerns will resurface. So we should not think that we could have accounting principles for the financial sector different from those applied to the non-financial sectors. As the Vice-President of the Spanish SEC, F. Restoy, stated (2008), "Using prudential policy tools would seem a more efficient way to address financial stability concerns than distorting the criteria used to report financial information." We thank Rafael Repullo for this reference.

capacity to hold the assets to maturity. It seems to us that this approach, increasingly adopted, would worsen one of the main problems of pro-cyclicality, which is that bankers and investors pay insufficient attention in the boom to the possibility that prices may fall back when the boom is over. Moreover, it does not strike us as credible for a bank to declare in the middle of a crisis that it is their intention to hold an asset to maturity and so it is no longer necessary to value it using current market prices, if the asset is funded using short-term money market borrowing that has dried up or is likely to do so before the asset matures. At the minimum this is not responsive to the increased demands of transparency that accompany the confusion of a crisis.

We believe that there is an adjustment to the mark-to-market approach, that better reflects the prudential interests of financial firms, will limit liquidity-sapping forced sales of assets where there is no funding difficulty, and is more honest than a suspension of market-to-market or a wholesale shift of assets to 'hold to maturity'. The approach is called mark-to-funding,[45] and the principle is that assets should be valued and managed , not according to the intention of the holder , but according to the funding capacity of the holder. Capacity to hold on to assets is driven by the maturity of the funding of the asset. In other words, if a bank has funded its twenty-year assets with one-month or shorter-term borrowings, then whatever their intention, they should value the asset using current market prices. If, however, the asset is funded with the issuance of a 10-year bond, the asset can be valued by a third party valuer (to ensure against fraudulent valuations) on the basis of the present value of the likely average price over the next ten years. In particular, this long-run valuation can place less weight on current daily price volatility and more on valuing the expected cash flows over the next ten years. This valuation exercise would be best carried out on the basis of pools of assets and pools of funding and not on an individual asset by asset basis.

If a bank is funded over the short-term, this approach will provide no more relief and would be no less pro-cyclical than mark-to-market value accounting. However, this would be a fair reflection of the price risk the firm faces if funding is not rolled over. If, however, a bank held a pool of long-term assets to which it could ascribe a pool of long-term funding then it would not be forced to sell an asset the bank considered good value over the time-horizon of its funding, merely because of daily price changes.

The counter-argument, of course, is that a bank cannot ascribe a particular pool of liabilities to a pool of particular assets, since all liabilities indistinguishably and pari passu finance all assets equivalently. We explore a way in which such a 'carve-out', whereby a specific pool of assets could be related to a specific pool of liabilities, could be undertaken in Box 1.

This approach would reduce sales of assets, caused by no other reason than changes in value accounting over a time period that is of little economic relevance to the way the asset is funded. If regulators emphasise short-term valuations irrespective of the funding of assets, the financial system's natural risk absorbers – those with long term funding or liabilities who can diversify current risks over time – will not be able to act in that capacity, thereby reducing the financial system's natural resilience. We would be left with an over-reliance on short-term

45 See Persaud (2008a, 2008c).

Box 1 Mark-to-funding: an exposition

There are two principal methods for valuing an asset. The first is its current market valuation, or an estimate of what that might be. The second is the present value of the (estimated) future cash flows from that asset. Normally arbitrage in the market forces these two alternative methods of valuation into close alignment; but sometimes liquidity risks, and other causes of market dysfunctionality, causes these two alternative approaches to diverge, occasionally sharply so, as in the case of mortgage-backed assets in the current crisis. It is our thesis that the choice of valuation methods in such cases should be based on the relative maturity of the intermediary's funding.

In order to illustrate the case most simply, assume that there are two banks, A and B. Both hold a single identical asset, whose market value has fallen well below the present value of future expected cash flows. Bank A has financed this asset on the basis of a long duration liability, (where the durations of asset and liability are exactly matched); whereas bank B has financed the same asset on the basis of a short-dated (one period) liability which needs to be rolled over each period. If the assets in both banks (A and B) are valued equally at the latest market price, both will appear to be insolvent. This is unfair to bank A, which has no need to sell the asset, and can ride out the liquidity (market) crisis, garnering the cash flows in due course. If, on the other hand, the assets in both banks are valued at the present value of expected cash flows, both may appear to be sound, but this too is incorrect, since the liquidity crisis means that bank B may either not be able to roll over its funding needs at all, or only at a much higher rate of interest. Bank B really is insolvent. Clearly there is a major difference in their solvency, depending on their relative funding positions, and the accounting methods ought to reflect this.

Apart from those who would deny that market prices can ever move away from the fundamentals of the P.V. of expected future cash flows, the above analysis should not be controversial. The problem that many see with mark to funding, instead, is practical. The above example was purposefully simplified with each bank having just one asset financed by one liability. In practice banks have n assets financed by j different forms of funding, where both n and j are large numbers. It is not possible normally to say that a particular liability finances a particular asset; instead all liabilities go into a common pot to finance all assets. On this view, although the objectives of mark-to-funding may be praiseworthy, it cannot be done in practice.

We think that this objection can be met. There are cases where particular assets and liabilities can be directly related, covered bonds and pfandbriefe being examples. Moreover occasions when P.V.s and market prices diverge significantly are likely to be quite rare. In practice our proposal would allow a bank, when such a divergence did occur, to 'carve out' the assets to which this applied, and to select which liabilities it chose from its portfolio to support those assets. Suppose that the chosen liabilities had as long a duration as the assets, then the valuation would be P.V; if half as long, then the valuation would be half P.V. ...

Box 1 contd.

...and half market price. In the figure below we show how the valuation would be done for a carve out involving two assets backed by three types of liability, but the principle could be extended to any number of assets and liabilities.

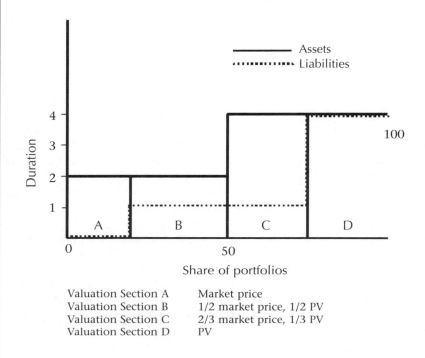

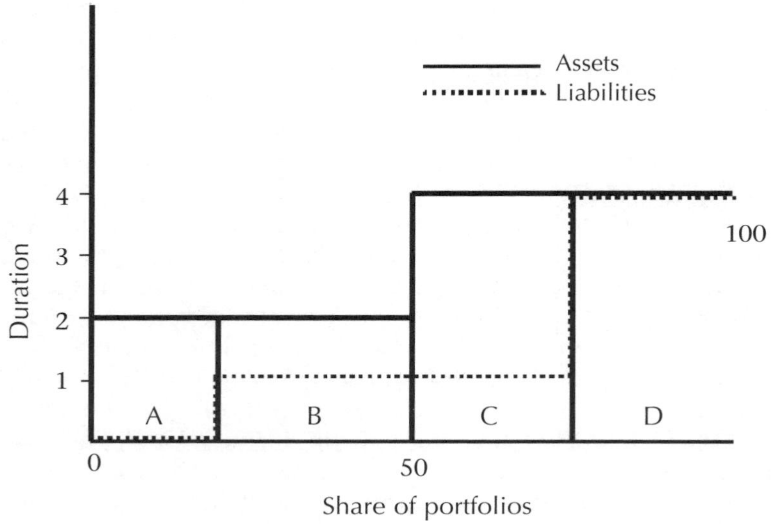

Valuation Section A	Market price
Valuation Section B	1/2 market price, 1/2 PV
Valuation Section C	2/3 market price, 1/3 PV
Valuation Section D	PV

If there was such a 'carve-out', the assets and liabilities involved would be excluded from the rest of the balance sheet, i.e. any subordinated debt used in such a 'carve out' could not be used also to satisfy tier 2 of Basel II, the assets/liabilities in the 'carve out' would cease to be calculated in the estimates of liquidity mis-match in the remainder of the portfolio; an exception would be that the carve-out would still figure towards the overall estimated leverage ratio.

In a sense what this proposal does is to allow any bank in a liquidity crisis to set up its own internal 'bad bank' mechanism so long as it has sufficient long term funding to support that. The need for such a mechanism should only be occasional, but a benefit of doing this is that it should provide an additional incentive for banks to seek out additional longer term funding in normal times.

Such a carve out could be operated flexibly with no limit on the use of assets or liabilities assigned to it, which could vary over time. Recall that the exercise would only come into operation when the P.V. of expected cash flows was significantly greater than the current market value of the assets involved. But...

Box 1 contd.

...such a mechanism might have been very beneficial to such banks as had a sufficiency of longer dated liabilities in the recent crisis.

In general, the current value accounting system discourages banks from long-term funding. The reward to a bank of lengthening the maturity of its funding is that it provides greater time with which to diversify risks. But this is lost if assets are valued as if they were to be sold tomorrow. It should be no surprise that banks have responded by relying on cheaper short-term funding, but as we have discussed above, this is risky both from the perspective of an individual bank and of the financial system. Mark-to-funding would enable banks to capture the reduction of risk associated with longer-term funding and would remove this artificial disincentive. Our proposal to charge capital for significant maturity mismatches in the funding of long-term assets should also augment this. Where banks have long-term funding, mark-to-funding would allow them to reflect the real risks facing them, and not to add to their own and systemic risks by forcing them to behave as if they actually have short-term funding. In this regard, mark-to-funding is in the spirit of a true and fair reflection of the financial conditions facing a bank.

funding and risk traders. Risk traders are those with limited capacity to diversify risks through time because of their capital or funding and whose risk management strategy is, effectively, to reduce risks when they rise by selling them on to someone else reduced (see Persaud, 2008b).

Some worry about the same asset being valued differently by different institutions. Of course this is already done within the financial sector as a whole. There are assets held by insurance companies that are valued on a hold-to-maturity basis that are also held by banks and valued on a mark-to-market basis and accepted reasoning is that an insurance company's liabilities are longer-term. Mark-to-funding merely extends and reinforces this approach along less ad hoc lines than is currently the case with 'Level 3' assets or assets currently held in non-mark-to-market regimes more generally.

Let us conclude our discussion on mark-to-funding with two caveats. First, while mark-to-funding will reduce the degree of market illiquidity caused by forced sales that would not have occurred were it not for a valuation and risk horizon that is not relevant to the asset holding, we are aware that most banks are in fact funded over the short-term. Of course, the adoption of mark-to-funding may also encourage financial institutions with long-term funding to be buyers of distressed assets, which will also support market liquidity.

The second caveat is that allowing 'hold-to-funding account' grants financial institutions some discretion how to value assets. This introduces additional asymmetric information and might hinder future funding. There are those who argue that fair value accounting is as arbitrary a valuation of a long-term asset, (or liabilities; many feel uncomfortable when a bank reduces losses/raises profits by writing down the value of its supposedly par-value liabilities because credit risk leads them to be traded at a discount, see amongst others, Buiter 2009), as any other, but to overcome the asymmetric information problem we would recommend that where assets are not valued on a mark-to-market basis, they will have to be valued by a third party and we would also subscribe to Allen and Carletti (2008) proposal that each financial institution should publish two balance sheets: one based on mark-to-funding and another one based on mark-to-market evaluations.

5.4 Capital charges against illiquidity

Our second proposed measure to reduce liquidity risk is to impose a capital charge on it. Conceptually, regulatory capital should be set aside against the riskiness of the combination of an asset and its funding, since the riskiness of an asset depends to a large extent on the way it is funded. The goal of our objective of this liquidity adjusted capital charges is to reduce funding liquidity risk by encouraging banks to find long-term funding, and dissuade them from greater leverage.

Let us first consider the wider merits of this principle before returning to more practical issues of estimating regulatory capital, since there will be many ways of applying this principle and the precise methodology of application is less important than the principle. The principle is in fact quite close in spirit to the mismatch ladder that had been considered by the Basle Committee a couple of decades ago.

To adopt the Basle language, if capital is to be risk sensitive, it must be sensitive not just to the risk of assets, but to the risk of the combination of the asset and its funding, which includes the leverage and maturity mismatch. We argue that if two banks hold the same asset, the one funding the asset with term deposits would set aside a lower amount of capital than the one funding the assets with overnight borrowing from the money markets. If funding markets dried up for three months, the short-term funded bank would be in difficulty and would be forced to sell assets that would worsen the liquidity and solvency environment for its competitors. The bank would cause a fire-sale externality due to low market liquidity.

In practical terms, adjustments to capital to reflect the maturity mis-match between assets and liabilities could be done as simple multiples to the current requirements for capital which are based on the credit quality of assets. If the boundary lines of regulation are recast as we suggest in Section 4, the multiples could have a minimum below 1.0, allowing this new capital requirement to be applied to institutions that have assets funded by long-term capital and enabling them to put aside less capital than those who fund assets by borrowing.

We could have a completely separate charge but we would prefer to integrate the liquidity 'charge' with the existing capital charge through the multiple for three reasons. First we feel that this would make it easier to adopt given the existing capital adequacy regime. Second, liquidity is a concern in cases where credit risk is an issue and so it makes sense that we are focused on the liquidity of 'risky' assets. It has been suggested that combining two error-prone measures, capital adequacy and a liquidity multiple, compounds the individual errors, but that is only the case should there be a strong positive correlation of the errors of both measures; it is probable that the errors are in fact negatively correlated. Greatest maturity mis-matches of assets and liabilities – our measure of systemic liquidity – tend to be seen at the height of a boom when the current capital adequacy estimates are likely to underestimate risk.

Others have argued that we place too much weight on time- and state-varying capital requirements; and yet others have proposed that banks could insure against liquidity shortages, for example Perotti and Suarez (2009). Clearly such insurances would have to be provided by the public sector, since only the Central Bank can provide sufficient liquidity in a crisis. In our view the premia that a Central Bank should levy should relate to a measure of maturity mismatch, so there could be an identical precuniary sanction whichever route was chosen. The difference would be that our proposal would also impinge on the required quantum of capital, whereas the insurance proposal would not. We regard the effective difference between the two proposals as minor.

We propose that the maturity mismatch multiple is a function of the months of *effective mismatch* between the asset maturity and the funding maturity. Estimating the effective funding maturity is marginally easier than estimating the effective asset maturity. It largely relates to the term of the borrowing. An issue arises where funding is through deposits which tend to be effectively long-term funding, but depositors often have instant access. In this case banks could be given an opportunity to prove to their supervisor that the effective maturity of their deposits is longer than a day, perhaps using past deposit behaviour in stressed environments as evidence[46].

The effective maturity of an asset takes the asset's market liquidity into account. We take as effective maturity of an asset to be the lower of the maturity of a loan[47] and the length of time it would take to sell the asset in a stressed environment without taking a significant haircut. Assets that are accepted by the central bank as collateral for loans without a significant hair cut would have an asset maturity of less than one day. One month loans have an asset maturity of a month or less.

The problem is assessing the effective maturity for long-term loans that are not (normally) eligible as collateral at the central bank. In the current stressed environment, assets that were previously considered highly liquid are being sold with large haircuts. In the circumstances were the maturity of loans are in excess of two years, supervisors can apply a default range of 12 to 24 months and require banks to put 50% of their assets in a 12 month bucket and 50% in a 24 month bucket to be reviewed periodically. If we had not previously proposed counter-cyclical multiples to the existing capital charge (see Section 4) we would also recommend regulators to raise the proportion of assets held in the 24 month bucket in a methodical manner as a boom progresses to act as a counter-cyclical measure.

If an asset can be sold to the central bank in a day and is funded with overnight borrowing, there is no maturity mismatch. On the other hand, if a twenty year mortgage may be sold in approximately 24 months, and is funded with overnight money, there is a significant maturity mis-match.

In our judgement, a reasonable range for the multiple might be 0.5 to 2.0, with a maturity mismatch of somewhere between 6 months carrying a multiple of 1.0.

46 It should be noted that where banks have attracted deposits through above normal interest rates, they appear to have captured the more footloose depositors who are quicker to depart at the first sight of trouble. Perhaps a measure of the longevity of the deposit is how poor the competitive interest rate is, a Divisia approach.

47 For assets other than loans we measure measured as the average time it takes to be paid back the current value of the asset.

The current crisis inevitably calibrates our sense of what is an adequate degree of safety. Ten years ago, ensuring that funding maturities would allow institutions to survive a few weeks in the face of a disruption to money markets was considered adequate. In the 2007-08 crisis, wholesale money markets have been more or less closed for many borrowers for over a year.

Finally, each bank can calculate its effective maturity mismatch for the whole balance sheet or also for several subpools. That is, capital could be assessed against pools of assets that have been assigned to pools of funding, as described in Box 5.1. The assignment of pools of funding can be changed as long as the capital requirement is then re-assessed. It is better to allow banks to form pools explicitly on their balance-sheets rather than give them the incentives to do it via off-balance sheet vehicles.

We recognise that estimating this liquidity multiple appears ad hoc. What is required, and what we have tried to map out, is a framework for assessing the liquidity risk (the effective maturity mis-match of pools of assets and corresponding pools of funding). It has been suggested that liquidity buffers would be simpler and they do appear so, but only by making the calibration process more subjective than we have done here.

As always in regulation, there are issues to be faced concerning home/host responsibilities. Traditionally regulation of liquidity has been the responsibility of the host country, at least in the case of subsidiaries. Subsidiaries can, and do, apply to the host country central bank for liquidity assistance. On the other hand, centralisation of (and economising on) liquid assets has been a key aspect of cross-border banking. That conflict of interest was, until recently, camouflaged by the willingness of regulators to dispense with controls over liquidity.

But now that conflict is resurfacing, for example in the FSA's requirement in the UK that all banks, including foreign-owned subsidiaries, hold specified ratios of British public sector debt. We would propose relating such liquidity ratios only to those foreign-owned subsidiaries designated as 'systemic' (see Section 3). Beyond that, we would suggest that, whereas the host country retains the prime responsibility for liquidity requirements, this can, and should, be modified by bilateral, or multi-lateral MOUs, perhaps in Europe through the good offices of CEBS.

6 Other Regulatory Issues

6.1 Introduction

Capital and liquidity requirements are the main staple of financial regulation. Nevertheless there are a number of other issues that need some discussion, though in some cases only briefly.

A major focus of public anger has been the huge remuneration of senior banking officials, who now appear to have reaped inappropriate pecuniary benefits for taking risks that others have ended up shouldering. Moreover, did the structure of such a reward system itself induce these same executives knowingly to take enhanced risk? We discuss this in sub-section 6.2.

The boom-bust cycle in the housing market has been closely associated with the credit cycle amongst the banks. In sub-section 6.3 we ask whether another instrument that the authorities might use to dampen down such cycles could be (counter-cyclical) variations in Loan-to-Value (LTV) or loan-to-income ratios.

We touch, briefly, on issues relating to Credit Rating Agencies, in sub-section 6.4, before concluding with short comments on Central Clearing Houses for derivatives, and the need to dampen end-year (and end-quarter) spikes in financial markets (sub-section 6.5 and 6.6).

6.2 Remuneration

Compensation practices at financial firms have become a topic of particular scrutiny in recent years. The general public has become increasingly aware of the high levels of remuneration in the financial sector and indignant when large severance packages are awarded to executives who have presided over meltdowns in franchise values. Both regulators and practitioners have recognized the potential for perverse incentives to lead to unjustified risk taking and thus to contribute to systemic instability. Political leaders, most recently at the G20 summit, have called for a reexamination of the incentive structure of compensation in the financial sector.

One benefit of a crisis is that it prompts action to deal with vulnerabilities that have been allowed to build up over an extended period of benign conditions. The drawback, however, is that hasty responses can have unintended consequences, and can focus on issues that have the greatest public profile, as opposed to the most significant practical impact.

The high level of public interest in the subject, combined with the financial turmoil of the current crisis means that some additional regulation of financial sector pay is inevitable.[48]

In what follows, we attempt to separate which pay practices are a legitimate subject for financial regulation and which are not. In line with the rest of this report, we focus primarily on issues that are directly associated with financial stability.

We do not believe that a public perception that financial sector salaries are 'too high' is a sufficient reason for regulation. A free market system generates wages and prices determined through the interaction of supply and demand. Unless there are reasons to believe that these forces are artificially distorted, in which case, as we argue below, there is a case for public intervention, trying to control pay is usually ineffective and frequently counterproductive.[49] Markets are adept at finding ways around regulations that attempt to fix wages and prices at levels that do not correspond to market equilibrium.

This is not to say there is no public policy interest in dealing with pay disparities. Far from it. Societies have devised numerous techniques to address the issue of income inequality, including most importantly the progressive income tax. The absolute level of pay in the financial sector, insofar as it raises social issues related to income disparities, should be dealt with by these mechanisms. In this respect, finance is no different from any other economic sector

There are, however, two aspects of financial sector pay that are legitimate objects of regulatory intervention. One relates to conflicts of interest and stakeholder protection, and the other relates to systemic stability.

Throughout our report, however, we are in essence talking about social externalities which for a host of reasons are not sufficiently internalized by banks. Bankers' remuneration has incorporated insufficient internalizing of the social costs of excessive lending. But we aim to deal with this through our additional capital charges. The response of banks to less profits in the boom should be smaller bonuses, so there would be less need for regulators to meddle in the overall level of remuneration.

Stakeholder protection issues arise when asymmetric information leads to levels of remuneration that depart from those that would prevail in a genuinely free market for talent. This can, in principle, occur when managers of businesses award themselves contracts that are more generous than the owners of the business would choose to award if they were aware of all the facts. The most immediate sufferers from such practices are the owners (shareholders) of the business, but insofar as excessive pay erodes the profitability of a financial firm, broader financial stability issues can also arise.

The answer to this potential distortion, we believe, lies in strengthened corpo-

---

48 To quote Thomas Huertas, Director of Banking Sector Regulation at the UK FSA:

> '...Supervisors will tackle remuneration policies. Firms themselves have admitted that remuneration policies may have been a contributory factor to the financial crisis. We concur, and have therefore written to the CEOs of major firms to assure that firms' remuneration policies are consistent with sound risk management. We will also work with other regulators in bodies such as the Financial Stability Forum to assure that this problem is tackled on a global basis'.

49 Regulators appear to agree with this assessment. To quote Thomas Huertas again: 'Our concern is not with the level of pay. We have no objection to people earning high compensation, provided they earn it in a way that is consistent with sound risk management...'.

rate governance. Boards of directors should have compensation committees that are appropriately reflective of shareholder interests. This means, at a minimum, that such committees should be composed of independent directors, with the capacity to reach informed judgments on pay levels and structures. We believe that transparency is also a valuable safeguard. Membership in Compensation Committees should be disclosed, and salaries and benefit levels for all senior executives should be made public.

To address the suspicion that compensation consultants play a role in ratcheting compensation levels upward, there could also be a case for requiring advice of compensation consultants to be divulged more widely. We believe that the supervisory authorities responsible for conduct of business regulation should formulate guidelines consistent with these principles and hold regulated institutions to account if they do not follow them.

Of much more moment from our perspective, however, is the potential for remuneration practices to adversely affect *systemic stability*. This will occur if the structure of remuneration encourages decision makers to take risks whose social costs diverge from the costs facing the individual decision taker. It is not hard to think of ways in which this could happen. Where a financial sector decision taker receives a portion of the profits generated in any time period, but does not absorb a corresponding share in the losses generated in other time periods, he/she has an incentive to take additional risks. The executive will obtain potentially large returns in good times, while simply receiving nothing in bad times.

There is a widespread belief that that was a general feature of remuneration packages in the period leading up to the present crisis, though quantified evidence is difficult to come by. It is certainly true that a number of company CEOs received large pay packages during the expansion phase and were not required to give back their gains when their companies ran into difficulties. Indeed, in a number of cases, it was reported that they received additional large severance packages when they were eventually forced to leave their positions. What is not known, however, is what impact this had on incentives for risk-taking, or how much of the remuneration was in forms that imposed losses on the recipient when stock prices plummeted.

How can society protect itself against the systemic consequences of distorted incentives in compensation structures? It can be argued that the first line of defense is companies' own self-interest. It is hard to believe that financial firms knowingly encourage excessive risk-taking. They presumably try to set up incentive structures that limit perverse incentives. And competitive pressures should ensure that the firms that are most successful in doing this are the long-term survivors. To some extent this happens, but the mechanism is self evidently insufficient, for at least two reasons.

First, it is very difficult for the owners of firms (ie shareholders) to effectively monitor the incentives facing managers. They do not have the information or expertise. And in a protracted period of good times, it is far from clear how risky certain activities actually are. So the shareholders of a firm are insufficiently aware of the risks being run by senior management, and senior management in turn may be insufficiently aware of the risks being run by the bankers and traders whose activities they oversee.

The *second* reason why it is not possible to rely simply on the self-interest of firms' owners is that the costs of an individual company's failure will understate the social costs, for reasons developed elsewhere in this report. The failure of one financial institution typically weakens the position of all others and brings the prospect of systemic meltdown closer.

For both of these reasons, we accept that there is an *a priori* case for supervisory intervention in the field of compensation practices. But what form should such intervention take? There is a clear risk of unintended consequences in subjecting compensation practices to regulation based on political pressure and public opinion. If the consequence is to constrain salaries below market clearing levels, then practices will spring up that evade the constraints. An example is the law introduced in the US in the 1990s that excluded salary payments in excess of $1 million per year from expenses deductible for tax purposes. The consequence was the development of incentive compensation techniques (such as payment in restricted stock and options) that rendered the intended salary restraint ineffective, and that had their own perversities.

So the question is what kinds of regulatory rules or guidelines would improve the incentive structure of executive pay in the financial sector. We consider here five possible techniques:

The *first* relates to the way in which bonuses are paid. It should be feasible to require delayed payment of bonuses, to mandate the greater use of payment in company stock, and to require the vesting of this stock for longer periods. We support these techniques, particularly for senior executives whose decisions affect the overall health of the company. But we caution that too much should not be expected of these reforms. Many, indeed most, financial companies, have followed such practices for quite a long time.

A *second* technique relates to the way in which bonuses are calculated. Employee incentive compensation should be tied strictly to risk-adjusted returns. Here too, however, it would be a mistake to expect too much. Most companies already attempt to measure risk-adjusted returns: the problem lies in the difficulties of calculating risk. Measured risk usually seems low at the height of a boom so that actual risk is underestimated. Moreover, even if traders are rewarded on a risk-adjusted basis, they may still have an incentive to take excessive risk. Systemic risk is something that materializes only infrequently. Traders and others will benefit from taking excessive risk in all the years when risk does not materialize, and will not suffer corresponding loss in years when major reverses occur.

A *third* approach attempts to equalize the balance of returns and losses through 'claw-back' provisions in bonus awards. Bonus payments could be placed in an escrow account, and only released after a suitable period had passed, during which no losses had been recorded. If such losses did occur, the employees claims on the compensation balance held in escrow would be reduced accordingly. As economists, this appeals to us on incentive grounds, though we doubt its practicality and even its legal enforceability. Since such provisions would obviously be unattractive to employees, the consequence would presumably be even higher bonuses to compensate for the attendant uncertainty.

A *fourth* approach is to reduce the incentive for risk taking by individual decision takers. For example, it has been suggested that bonuses should be based on firm-wide performance, rather than the performance of individuals or their business units. We have some doubts about the effectiveness and desirability of this.

It would certainly reduce the incentive to take risks in individual activities. But it would largely undermine the purpose of incentive pay. Furthermore, it might appear inequitable in a multi-functional firm, if employees in a business unit that was successful had their pay reduced because of the less successful activities of another business unit. It may even lead to the emergence of smaller, more specialized firms that would do little to change systemically dangerous behaviour, but would make the financial system even harder to observe.

The *fifth* approach seeks to utilize the checks and balances of corporate governance to bring individual and corporate interests into better alignment. Internal compensation committees could be required to have risk control staff as ex officio members, and such staff could be given veto powers over compensation structures deemed to be too risky.

In what form should regulation over pay be introduced? We have elsewhere expressed a preference for 'bright line' rules that limit supervisory discretion, on the grounds that it is hard for supervisors to impose discretionary rules in times of general euphoria. In the case of compensation, however, we see little alternative but to rely on a measure of supervisory discretion. We believe that supervisors should formulate a set of remuneration guidelines, based on the principles set out above, and assess the degree of compliance of each supervised institution. Using a relatively simple scale (eg. 'fully compliant', 'largely compliant' and 'partially compliant', (which could be published) automatic adjustments would be made to capital ratios. Those institutions that were judged to have compensation practices that failed to restrain excessive risk taking would therefore pay a penalty in additional required capital.

6.3 Loan-to-value ratios in mortgages

The epicentre of the financial crisis occurred in the housing market, especially, but not only, in the USA and UK. The boom/bust cycle was exacerbated by the conditions for mortgage lending becoming ever easier in the boom and tightening in the bust. This was particularly so for loan-to-value (LTV) ratios. Time and state-varying LTVs have been used successfully in countries such as Estonia and Hong Kong.

They can, however, be easily avoided in most circumstances by taking out second mortgages or routing the mortgage borrowing abroad. Such avoidance can be discouraged, as is done in several European countries, by limiting the right of a lender to repossess property to first liens recorded in a register kept within the country. So second secured mortgages can be prevented as well as first mortgages made abroad, but not recorded locally, since they would be, in effect, unsecured.

Resort to legal prohibition in this fashion is undesirable. Nevertheless the impetus to the housing cycle caused by the competitive ratching up of LTVs in the boom (often to 100+, e.g. Northern Rock), and their abrupt decline (often to around 75%) in the bust, has been large. The lesser evil may be for the Central Bank to set a maximum LTV, say 90%, and even to lower it should house price increases appear to be getting out of hand. Canadian law, for example, specifies a maximum LTV (80%) and the mortgage must be on the principal residence.

More generally, the US regulators are proposing the creation of a separate mortgage origination authority that would set standards for such origination. We believe this would be a valuable innovation, that could usefully be copied by other countries. Appropriate mortgage origination standards would curb abuses and limit the extent to which unqualified buyers were enabled to bid up housing prices on the basis of lax lending standards. There are also other aspects of US, and other country, mortgage markets that could benefit from reconsideration, for example moving away from non-recourse mortgages and interest deductability.

6.4 Credit rating agencies

Credit Rating Agencies have lost much of their reputation in this crisis, mainly as a result of giving high initial ratings to securitized mortgage-backed securities that after the event appear to have been wrong. They are widely accused of nefarious behaviour, notably via a conflict of interest, since they get paid by the issuers of securities (the sell side), who naturally want higher ratings. We tend to think that this particular criticism is exaggerated. Credit rating agencies have a franchise value that depends on objective opinions. This would be undermined if they were known to shade their assessment in order to gain business.

What is of greater concern is the conflict of interest that arises in the advisory business of CRAs. The advisory arms of CRAs help potential issuers structure offers in such a way as to gain a desired rating. Having advised an issuer on debt structure, it is hardly likely that the rating arm of the CRA would fail to grant the promised rating. We therefore favour the legal separation of ratings business from ratings advisory services. We also favour enhanced transparency about the way in which CRAs assess the creditworthiness of structured products. What we do not favour, however, is formal oversight of the ratings process. This would, we believe, tend to give too much of an official endorsement to ratings.

Rather than accusing CRAs of sharp practice, our view is rather that the CRAs failed to appreciate the likelihood that US housing prices might decline across the board, and the extent that probabilities of default could migrate upwards in that event. Most forecasters have had poor, chequered records over the last two years. CRAs are just another group of forecasters, and they have done just as badly.

Anyhow, whether the CRAs were knaves (conflict of interest) or fools (poor forecasters, like most other forecasters), the question is what to do about their role in the general conduct of regulation. Tightening up, yet further, on potential conflicts of interest,[50] and, yet more, transparency in both methods and results is all very well; the greater problem is that the ratings provided by (fallible) CRAs, using fallible models, have been placed at the centre of the regulatory process itself, for example the Basel II Standardised Approach. And given the strategic behaviour that rating disclosures can generate, placing CRAs at the centre of regulation may have added to their fallibility.

In this latter regard there are two alternative generic approaches. The first is to remove CRAs and their ratings as far as possible from the structure of formal regulation altogether. Investment managers and bankers should take responsibility for their own decisions, and they (and their regulators) should no more be allowed

50 The worse conflict is in their consultancy and advisory activity.

to hide behind CRA forecasts than, for example, behind government forecasts of future growth.

The alternative, second, approach is to register and to regulate the CRAs, but to leave them with a central role in the regulatory process.

Our preference is for the first approach. Regulation will not make the CRAs forecast better; but will mean that the authorities will be conjoined in the resulting condemnation as and when the CRAs get it wrong in future, as they inevitably will. Moreover, governments are themselves large-scale issuers of debt. Might government regulation trespass on the (fragile) independence of CRAs when it comes to rating such debt?

6.5 Centralized clearing house arrangements vs. OTC markets

Certain financial markets are systemic in the sense that their closure or malfunction would cause adverse externalities and contagion. As a general matter what is needed is a centralized clearing house (CCH) in any such systemic market, to lessen the risk that the failure, or anticipated failure, of a counter-party might cause widespread financial problems; the CCH should have the power to determine and to adjust the conditions for trading, e.g. margin requirements.[51] In particular, when a market grows to a size when it becomes systemic, such as the Credit Default Swap (CDS) market, the relevant authorities should have the powers to require an Over the Counter (OTC) bilateral and unregulated market to be reshaped into a centralized, regulated market. Reforming, and improving the regulation of, the market infrastructure of the financial system, centralized counter parties for systemic markets, improving the clearing, settlement and payment systems, remains a key element in the whole exercise of reconstructing the regulation of the financial system.

While there are substantial benefits in centralizing the clearing and settlement processes of systemically important markets, we are less convinced that all OTC contracts should be forced on to an exchange. There are legitimate institutional difficulties in a market organizing a centralized clearing facility, but there are many trading venues and exchanges and we have some respect for the revealed preference for some instruments to trade off an exchange and some on, especially where there are idiosyncratic contracts. We believe the mechanism of differential capital haircuts could be used to shift a large proportion of relevant transactions onto regulated exchanges, while allowing the flexibility of OTC contracts where these are economically justified.

6.6 Year-end spikes

Finally, quite a lot of the pressure to maintain adequate liquidity concentrates on the presentation of an end-year balance sheet, with minor spikes at the half-year and end-quarter. Concerns about end-year positions typically cast their shadow

51 See Brunnermeier (2009) for a theoretical explanation how network effects in over the counter-market arrangements can lead to adverse amplifications.

forward into the late autumn for weeks, if not months ahead. Each institution wants to window-dress their published end-year figure to show a degree of liquidity that they do not feel the need for at other times.

That this should be allowed to disrupt, or threaten to disrupt, financial systems appears absurd. There are several potential remedies. The institutions could be required to report an average figure, (over the last quarter), taken at monthly or weekly observations. Alternatively, the authorities could just facilitate whatever window-dressing the institutions wanted by offering one-day repos on a massive scale. The resulting balance sheet would often hardly be 'fair and true', but the end-year spike is economically damaging, especially at a time of frayed nerves. Some solution needs to be found.

6.7 Crisis management

Each 'individually systemic' financial institution should be required to provide an annual contingency plan for dealing with its own bankruptcy. The contingency plan should include procedures how best to unwind existing positions and obligations. Special emphasis should be placed on the potential risk spillovers to other financial institutions and the economy as a whole.

7 The Structure of Regulation

A sensible maxim in this field is to defer delegation of responsibility to an institution for achieving some objective until, and unless, one can also equip that institution with sufficient powers and instruments to achieve that end. There has been some tendency in the past to allocate responsibility for financial stability to Central Banks without due consideration of what instruments they might use to achieve that objective.

The one instrument that they could wield, the short term interest rate, has been predicated to the achievement of (goods and services) inflation. The recent period of financial turmoil has raised queries whether the primary target of price stability should be widened to include asset prices. While we do suggest that an appropriate measure of housing prices should be in the price index used for the inflation target, we do believe that, wherever possible, a separate objective should be achieved by a separate instrument (the Tinbergen principle of relating instruments to targets). Thus the objective of financial stability should be achieved by the development and application of instruments designed for that purpose. Of course the use of either instrument, interest rates and macro-prudential regulatory measures, will affect the conjuncture in which the other operates. Indeed, in circumstances when quantitative easing is being used, the two instruments may merge to become almost indistinguishable. But we do not view this as a serious problem.

It has been a primary purpose of this paper, in sections 3 to 5 to sketch out macro-prudential instruments that can be used in this way. We like to think that we have proposed a sufficient armoury. An important question is the balance between discretion and rules in their application. The more that the utilisation of such instruments is likely to provoke opposition from major interest groups at the time of their application, the more such application needs to be based on pre-set, pre-announced, (even statutory) rules. 'Taking away the punch-bowl, just when the party gets going' is no more popular with respect to asset price booms, than to the macro-economic conjuncture. For this latter reason we would advocate that much of the counter-cyclical armoury that we have suggested becomes couched in presumptive, rule-based terms.

Throughout we have emphasized the differences between macro-prudential and micro-prudential regulatory measures. Such differences extend naturally to the ethos, discipline and cultures of the institutions involved. The macro-prudential institution should be macro, aggregate, systemic and economic in outlook; the micro-prudential institution(s) should be more micro, individual, prudential, legal and accounting-based. This is closely in accord with the US Treasury, 'Blueprint for

Modernized Financial Regulatory Structure', (March 2008). Naturally the macro institution will be the national Central Bank and the micro institution(s) will be one, or more, Financial Services Supervisory institutions.

It is, however, a mistake to channel all direct supervisory contact with the individual regulated financial intermediaries through the micro-prudential institution(s), as has been done in the UK. The macro-prudential body, in effect the Central Bank, needs to maintain direct links, including on-site supervision when required, with all those institutions designated as 'systemic' and also with those which the Central Bank suspects may be becoming systemic. We repeat, and support, the concluding principal 'observation' (observation 9) of the G-30 (2008) paper on 'The Structure of Financial Supervision' that 'Irrespective of structural approach, central banks everywhere express the critical importance of their having information about, and a direct relationship with, large systemically important financial institutions.'

In a sense what we are recommending is a reversion to the prior twin-peaks approach, with one peak being the macro, systemic, economic Central Bank, and the other being the micro, individual, prudential (and conduct of business), legal and accounting FSA. When the UK went for a unified, single peak, approach, there was no discussion of its advantages and disadvantages vis-à-vis the twin peaks approach. There should have been. The decision then was wrong, despite its apparent economising on scarce supervisory resources and its limitation on vexatious supervisory visits to the regulated. Macro and micro-prudential regulators/supervisors have essentially different viewpoints, and both are valid.

Dealing with the question of the structure of financial regulation within the individual nation state, however, is much easier than trying to review and to reform the international structure. Here we start with two considerations, indeed facts, that limit the application of an international level-playing-field. First asset price cycles, and the pace of credit expansion, differ between countries. So, counter-cyclical measures have to be applied by host countries to the (systemically important) financial institutions in their own countries. The inevitable implication is that, even though the principles of application may/should be the same across countries, the effective capital ratios applied to banks will differ depending on where their assets and liabilities are situated.

In our view, the ability to apply counter-cyclical regulation (both to capital and liquidity) implies, as its corollary, a shift of the balance of powers towards the host country, away from the home country, and also some departure from the level-playing-field ideal. The implication is that macro-prudential instruments would generally be wielded by the Central Bank of the host country, and micro-prudential instruments by the FSA of the home country on a consolidated basis. How serious a drawback this might be is a matter for discussion. The large cross-border financial intermediaries might be slightly inconvenienced[52] but does that matter that much if the purpose of the exercise is to tailor the regulatory countervailing pressures to the financial stability conditions within each country? This would, of course, have numerous structural implications, implying for example a less pressing need for 'colleges of regulators'.

---

52 Any potential additional burden on the regulated could, in principle, be offset by a redoubled effort to harmonize reporting requirements and definitions across countries

The second consideration, fact, that we would note is that crisis management is often very expensive, and that the main source of such funding clearly has to be national Treasuries, and ultimately the taxpayer.[53] He who pays the piper, calls the tune. So long as the Minister of Finance, and national taxpayers, are ultimately at risk of needing to pay out money from the results of regulatory failure, they will want to design and control their own regulatory and supervisory procedures, and rightly so.

But what about Europe, where the objective is a single financial system? Crisis management can be hugely expensive, as has been seen. As soon as, but not before, the federal centre gets the power to raise funds (ultimately via taxation) to undertake such crisis management, then supervision can be transferred to the federal centre, and the euro area run for regulatory and financial stability purposes as a single financial entity. Absent such a fiscal centralisation, which the authors of this paper would like to happen, the fiscal powers, crisis management, supervision and the protection of national financial systems remain at the nation state level, (as has been seen in practice in this crisis), and the design of regulation has to reflect this.[54]

Although crisis management has to be done at the nation state level, absent a shift of fiscal competence for this purpose to the supra-national region, there remain considerable useful opportunities for international cooperation in crisis prevention.

At present, international cooperation is carried on through a network of supervisory committees and through international organizations such as the BIS, the IMF and, particularly, the Financial Stability Forum (FSF). Sectoral supervisory committees have a history stretching back over thirty years. The Basel Committee on Banking Supervision was formed in 1974 under the aegis of the G10 central bank governors in the wake of the Herstatt crisis. Its original goal was to clarify the areas of responsibility of home and host supervisors where there was a failure of an internationally active bank. Subsequently, however, the Committee became the source of supervisory rule-making more generally. It is now best known for setting minimum capital standard for internationally active banks ('Basel I' and 'Basel II'). Although negotiated only among G10 regulators and central banks, these soon became global standards.

International cooperation in the securities and insurance fields took longer to crystallize, for both political and historical reasons. There was no 'crisis' in these sectors to force cooperation; there was no pre-existing body, such as the G10 central bank Governors' committee, to act as a convening authority; and the responsibility for insurance and securities regulation was generally more fragmented. Still, following the model of the banking regulators, cooperative committees of

53 The only source of international funding for crisis management is the IMF. But their available resources are relatively small, dwarfed in size by the funds recently applied in developed countries to recapitalise their own banking systems. Calls to give the IMF greater responsibilities have not been matched by measures to give them greater resources or other instruments of control. Without the latter, they cannot realistically assume the former.

54 The recent CEPS Task Force Report (December 1, 2008), on 'Concrete Steps towards More Integrated Financial Oversight', proposes using the European Investment Bank (EIR) for this purpose (Section 3.3). While we welcome their appreciation of this issue, we fear that the potential scale of fiscal requirement, as evidenced in the current crisis, could be well beyond the EIB's financial capacities, even if it were to call upon all its additional capital resources. Moreover, this would lead the EIB towards becoming the main regulatory authority; would that be a welcome development?

standard setters were set up by the International Organisation of Securities' Commissions (IOSCO) and the International Association of Insurance Supervisors (IAIS).

The need for a more formal international body to take overall responsibility for global financial stability, and to bring together the relevant national authorities, was recognized in the wake of the Asian crisis. The G7 ministers and governors established the FSF in 1999, comprising Central Bank Deputy Governors, Deputy Finance Ministers and heads of regulation from G7 countries, along with senior representatives of the main international institutions. Subsequently, participation was extended to a few countries outside the G7 with important financial markets. (The Chairman of the Forum is appointed in a personal capacity; one of the authors of this report served as the first Chairman).

Although the FSF has done much useful work, and established closer relationships among key regulatory authorities, it has suffered from several handicaps, which need to be addressed. We believe that, if these handicaps can be satisfactorily dealt with, the FSF could play a key role in a revised global regulatory environment.

A *first* problem with the FSF, as currently structured, is that it does not have formal representation from key emerging markets. This is partly because the original G7 wanted to retain their control over a process they believed affected primarily their own markets. It is also partly due to the desire to keep the number of participants manageable in order to promote confidential discussions within the Forum.. (Even with the current country membership, multiple participants from countries and IFIs means that there were some 35 people around the table.)

Initially, the FSF tried to balance the need for emerging market input and small-group discussions through regional meetings with key authorities in Asia, Latin America and Eastern Europe. This had some success but was eventually abandoned, partly because of pressure on key participants' time. We believe the time has now come to formally expand the membership of the FSF by adding participants from the main emerging markets. It seems that the political leadership of the G20, in its declaration following the November 2008 summit, accepts this logic. The difficult political task will be deciding exactly which countries should be invited to join.

A *second* institutional shortcoming of the current FSF lies in the multiple representation of the G7 countries (and to a lesser extent, of international organisations). The G7 countries have three representatives each, to accommodate the competing claims of finance ministries, central banks and regulatory agencies. Not only does this add to the numbers around the table and thus inhibit discussion, it dilutes responsibility. We believe the major economies should designate a single top-level participant from the agency with overarching responsibility for financial stability at the national level. This individual should preferably be the head of the agency and should become the sole representative of the country in the FSF. A similar limitation could be imposed on international organisations, such as the IMF and World Bank. If this were done, it should be possible to bring into the FSF all key emerging markets without expanding its size beyond what is consistent with frank and confidential round-table discussion.

A *third* problem for any international body is the tendency of national authorities and the general public to resist warnings of vulnerability during good times.

The FSF issued several warnings in the period leading up to the 2007 outbreak of turbulence, but these were not heeded. (A similar experience befell warnings issued by the IMF and BIS.) It is to deal with this tendency that we have advocated 'hard-wiring' counter-cyclical regulatory guidelines that we believe might be hard to implement through supervisory discretion.

Nobody can mandate that the advice of the Financial Stability Forum should be accepted by governments. But we believe techniques should be explored to underwrite the independence of judgments by the Forum and to ensure that its judgments are given adequate publicity.

A *fourth* problem that can be ameliorated but not completely solved is the fact that the legal basis of regulation is national, while financial institutions and markets global in scope. We do not believe that international legal authority, however desirable, is a practical political possibility in the foreseeable future. Nor do we think it is desirable to constrain the activities of financial institutions and markets within national boundaries. For this reason, there will inevitably be gaps and overlaps in regulation. Any practical approach to this problem must therefore focus on strengthening mechanisms of cooperation among independent national authorities.

Even more important than the internal governance mechanism of the FSF is what it should actually do. We see key functions in three areas: (i) crisis prevention, through ensuring stronger, more appropriate and more consistent prudential standards; (ii) crisis warning, through the monitoring and highlighting of systemic vulnerabilities, and (iii) crisis management, in cases where financial turmoil breaks out.

With regard to *crisis prevention*, there is no need to eliminate the current role of international standard setters in the areas of their individual responsibilities. In other words, the Basel Committee, perhaps with a revised membership, should continue to be the lead grouping for formulating cross-border banking standards; and similarly with IOSCO and the IAIS for the securities and insurance industries, and IASB for accounting standards. But the FSF should have the responsibility of opining on the consistency of proposed supervisory standards with overall systemic stability.

Elsewhere in this report, we have pointed out examples of where a focus on institutional (or microprudential) safety and soundness may not be sufficient to ensure system-wide (or macroprudential) stability. Indeed such a focus may even be counterproductive in this respect. We see one task of a revamped FSF as being to verify that rules proposed by standard setters are consistent with overall system-wide stability Subjecting the proposals of supervisory groupings to a 'consistency check' by a body such as the FSF could provide a useful mechanism to make sure that regulation does not become inadvertently procyclical.

With regard to *crisis warning*, the role we envisage for the FSF is not greatly different from the one it plays at the moment. But we do see a need for modifications to improve the chances that warnings do not go unheeded. One would be to give co-responsibility for early warnings to the IMF, enhancing the authority of the resulting judgments, and bringing in the IMF's macroeconomic expertise. To safeguard against political pressure to pull punches, Early Warning Reports should be produced under the authority of the Chairman of the FSF and the Managing Director of the IMF, without editing by member country representatives. With regard to the FSF's recommendations, countries would be asked to 'comply or explain' their responses.

Crisis resolution presents perhaps the greatest challenge. As already noted, crisis resolution usually involves fiscal resources and thus involves governments and parliaments. In the case of a financial crisis such as the one we are now experiencing, it is hard to see governments delegating this authority to an international organisation, or using domestic budgetary resources to help support the cross-border operations of foreign-based financial institutions. We recognise, therefore, that the best that can be expected is to use cooperative mechanisms, and existing discussion fora to improve information exchange and to promote negotiations on optimal resolution strategies.

The significance of this activity should not be minimised, however. Where there are global ramifications from a particular course of action, countries represented in the FSF should commit to avoid measures harmful to the interests of others. When a country is contemplating a measure to provide systemic support to its financial system, (for example, a guarantee of bank deposits) it should accept an obligation to inform partner countries of its intentions in advance of their implementation, and to provide for an adequate interval to consider the international implications of such actions. None of this, of course, would guarantee a cooperative outcome. But it would at least ensure that the mechanisms existed to permit such a resolution, if the political will was there.

8 Conclusions

The design of financial regulation is not straight-forward. When everyone is baying for more, tougher regulation, it is not needed, (because everyone is risk averse). When such regulation is badly needed, no one wants it, (since the good times are expected to roll on). This suggests that financial regulation should be focussed, primarily rule-based, (because discretion will be hard to use during periods of boom/euphoria), and time and state-varying (light during normal periods, increasing as systemic threats build up). The Spanish dynamic pre-provisioning scheme is about the only current instrument that meets these criteria.

Our analysis of the state of financial regulation leads on to quite a lengthy list of key points and recommendations which can be divided into four main headings, to wit General, Capital, Liquidity and Other.

8.1 General conclusions and recommendations (primarily from Chapters 1 and 2)

1. Regulation (external intervention) should always be capable of justification as a consequence of some specified market failure
2. The main cause of externalities arises because the social cost of systemic financial collapse exceeds the private cost to the individual financial institutions (and markets). A collapse of a financial institution causes risk spillovers. Effective regulation should provide incentives for financial institutions to internalize these externalities (risk spillovers).
3. The main cause of systemic collapse is endogenous risk, the likelihood of self-amplifying spirals like the loss and margin spiral.
4. Stress tests examine the responses of banks to exogenous risks. By construction they do not incorporate endogenous risk. Completely new techniques, perhaps based on models and endogenous risk-spillover measures, like CoVaR, need to be devised to explore the implications of endogenous risk for the system.
5. Requirements based on minimum capital ratios do not provide resilience, since they cannot be breached. They represent a burden to banks, not a source of strength.
6. Requirements should, instead, be normally restated in terms of higher target levels of capital, with a specific, statutory (i.e. not discretionary) and forceful ladder of increasing sanctions. This ladder should have a

minimum point at which either the deficiency is satisfactorily redressed, or the institution is shut down, i.e. prompt corrective action, p.c.a.

7. The response to the current crisis has led in several countries to a further concentration of the banking system and, perhaps, elsewhere amongst hedge funds. Greater intervention to encourage competition and to prevent oligopolistic behaviour may well be warranted.

8.2 Capital requirements (primarily from Chapters 3 and 4)

1. Banks, and any other financial institution subject to deposit insurance, should be subject to some (low) minimum capital requirement. This is not to be seen as a protection for the regulated institution (rather the reverse; it constrains the banks), but as a protection for the deposit insurance fund, and a trigger for p.c.a.
2. All regulators/supervisors in each country should agree their own list of systemic institutions and markets, and be prepared to exchange lists with supervisors in other countries. Although such lists should not be made public, (o.a. moral hazard and the fuzzy definition of 'systemic'), there should be mechanisms for ensuring that regulators/supervisors take this exercise most seriously.
3. All such systemic institutions should be subject both to micro-prudential regulation, examining their individual risk characteristics (along the lines of Basel II) and to macro-prudential regulation, related to their contribution to systemic risk. We suggest that this latter be done by adjusting the micro-prudential ratio by a co-efficient relating to the macro-prudential assessed risk.
4. Macro-prudential regulation should be countercyclical and lean especially against bubbles whose bursting can impair the financial intermediation sector.
5. We argue that the best measures of an institution's contribution to macro-prudential risk are its leverage, maturity mismatch and rate of expansion. More precise endogenous risk-spillover measures that also take liquidity aspects into account should be developed. So we would interact each, systemic, institution's tier 1 Basel II ratio by multiplicand, which could be below, as well as above, unity, based on a mixture of leverage, maturity mismatch and growth.
6. Institutions which are not individually systemic, but which are (i) highly leveraged with short-term debt and (ii) hold assets with low market liquidity (at times of a crisis), can nevertheless have systemic effects via joint herd-type behaviour. So they should all, except for the tinies, both report, and have some constraints (in the form again of a ladder of sanctions), on their macro-prudential riskiness, i.e. their leverage, maturity mismatch and credit expansion, (which could perhaps vary between kinds of institutions, e.g. banks and hedge funds).

   It would be for discussion, (and our group could not agree), whether such highly-leveraged, but individually non-systemic, institutions should also have *any* additional micro-prudential regulation.
7. Asset-price and credit cycles differ from country to country, and from

region to region. Although the principles of counter-cyclical regulation should be universal, its application would lead to differing ratios in each area applying the regulations, normally in the host country.

8. Each host country (region) should have the right to designate a cross-border subsidiary, or branch, as 'systemic'. Systemic branches should be required to become subsidiaries. Foreign-owned subsidiaries should be subject to the same capital requirement calculations, and hold that in domestic assets, as its own domestic banks.
9. An alternative approach, which might be less radical, would be to generalise and to extend the present Spanish dynamic pre-provisioning scheme to all countries, though this also would need to be applied on a country-by-country basis. If this were to be done, IFRS would have to be revised to permit this.
10. The application of macro-prudential measures should be by the Central Bank; for this purpose they should be able to undertake (on-site) supervision of individual systemic institutions, separately from the micro-prudential supervisor(s). Efforts should be made to limit the administrative burden of multiple supervisors, and reporting requirements and definitions should be harmonised.

8.3 Liquidity (primarily from Chapter 5)

1. We propose a 'mark to funding' approach to provide incentives for more long-term funding. This approach is, in effect, closely akin to the maturity mis-match ladder previously considered by the Basel Committee on Banking Supervision (BCBS) and by some Central Banks.
2. Unlike most such prior exercises we would also provide incentives to hold liquidity by, once again, interacting the assessed liquidity with the capital adequacy ratio. Liquidity is measured by an effective maturity mismatch which takes the market liquidity of assets (at times of crisis) into account. The more liquidity fell below the well-targeted level, the higher the CAR would have to be, and vice versa. The relationship (trade-off) need not, however, be linear.
3. We doubt whether additional private insurance can then help much on occasions when market and funding liquidity vanishes; the examples of the mono-lines and of AIG confirm our doubts. The answer would seem to be some combination of public sector market-making, (as now by the Fed in the CP market), and public sector insurance, (guarantees of one kind or another).
4. We suggest that mark-to-funding might be a principle that could apply to the portfolios of financial institutions for accounting purposes, either as an alternative, or a supplement, to the present categories, i.e. hold to maturity, available for sale, trading book.
5. To overcome debt overhang problems, the regulator should have the authority to convert such versions of existing debt, as already counts as tier 1 or tier 2 capital, into equity.

8.4 Other considerations (primarily from Chapters 6 and 7)

1. We propose that supervisors should formulate a set of remuneration guidelines, and, (as in other examples below), adjust capital ratios according to the degree of compliance.
2. We advocate the Central Bank setting maximum Loan-to-Value (LTV) ratios for residential mortgages as an additional macro-prudential measure. This would involve, as a corollary, outlawing several obvious avoidance measures, e.g. second mortgages.
3. We argue, at several points, that credit ratings are systematically misused in the regulatory process. Whereas we are happy to see further tightening of 'conflict-of-interest' and transparency regulations, we would otherwise seek to exclude CROs from the regulatory network altogether. We regard both the Basel II approach to the use of credit ratings and the European proposals for their enhanced regulation as misconceived.
4. We support the efforts of the CRMPG to move systemically important derivative markets onto centralised clearing houses.
5. Each 'individually systemic' financial institution should be required to provide annually a full contingency plan for dealing with its own bankruptcy.
6. We cannot understand how, and why, the end-year spike in financial markets has been allowed to remain. It is both absurd and damaging. We suggest two alternative methods of eradicating it.
7. Because cycles (in asset prices and credit) vary from country to country, as well as from time to time, we propose a shift of emphasis in regulatory powers towards the host country.
8. Because crisis management is often extremely expensive, it has to be done by the (host) Central Bank in conjunction with its own Ministry of Finance. As soon as, but not before, the euro area obtains fiscal powers to manage any such crises, *then* macro-prudential management can be shifted from the National Central Banks to some federal euro area body.
9. Whereas crisis management has to be done at a (national) level consonant with the availability of fiscal (taxpayer) funding, crisis prevention can, and should, be done internationally. We make several proposals to reform both the structure and remit of the Financial Stability Forum.

We have put forward nearly 30 key points and recommendations. If adopted, they would change the present system radically and for the better.

Appendix : The Boundary Problem in Financial Regulation

There are a number of fundamental, generic issues relating, at all times and everywhere (almost) to financial regulation. In particular if regulation is effective, it will constrain the regulated from achieving their preferred, unrestricted, position, often[55] by lowering their profitability and their return on capital. So the returns achievable within the regulated sector are likely to fall relative to those available on substitutes outside. There will be a switch of business from the regulated to the non-regulated sector. In order to protect their own businesses, those in the regulated sector will seek to open up connected operations in the non-regulated sector, in order to catch the better opportunities there. The example of commercial banks setting up associated conduits, SIVs and hedge funds in the last credit bubble is a case in point.

But this condition is quite general. One of the more common proposals, at least in the past,[56] for dealing with the various problems of financial regulation has been to try to limit deposit insurance and the safety net to a set of 'narrow banks', which would be constrained to hold only liquid and 'safe' assets. The idea is that this would provide safe deposits for the orphans and widows. Moreover, these narrow banks would run a clearing-house and keep the payments' system in operation, whatever happened elsewhere. For all other financial institutions outside the narrow banking system, it would be a case of 'caveat emptor'. They should be allowed to fail, without official support or taxpayer recapitalisation.

In fact, in the UK something akin to a narrow banking system was put in place in the 19th century with the Post Office Savings Bank and the Trustee Savings Bank. But the idea that the official safety net should have been restricted to POSB and TSB was never seriously entertained. Nor could it have been. When a 'narrow bank' is constrained to holding liquid, safe assets, it is simultaneously prevented from earning higher returns, and thus from offering as high interest rates, or other valuable services, (such as overdrafts), to its depositors. Nor could the authorities in good conscience prevent the broader banks from setting up their own clearing house. Thus the banking system outside the narrow banks would grow much faster under normal circumstances; it would provide most of the credit to the private sector, and participate in the key clearing and settlement processes in the

55 Though it keeps on being revisited; Telser, L.G. (2008) is a recent example.

56 This does not rule out any role for quasi-public utilities in the financial system. Public sector narrow banks, like POSB in the UK or Postfinance in Switzerland, can continue to provide useful services, especially if their services are priced appropriately. Also there can often be a role for a quasi-public sector utility in financial market infrastructures.

economy.[57]

This might be prevented by law, taking legal steps to prohibit broader banks from providing means of payment or establishing clearing and settlement systems of their own. There are, at least, four problems with such a move. First, it runs afoul of political economy considerations. As soon as a significant body of voters has an interest in the preservation of a class of financial intermediaries, they will demand, and receive, protection. Witness money market funds and 'breaking the buck' in the USA. Second, it is intrinsically illiberal. Third, it is often possible to get around such legal constraints, e.g. by having the broad bank pass all payment orders through an associated narrow bank. Fourth, the reasons for the authorities' concern with financial intermediaries, for better or worse, go well beyond insuring the maintenance of the basic payment system and the protection of small depositors. Neither Bear Stearns nor Fannie Mae had small depositors, or played an integral role in the basic payment system. Nevertheless, as has already been discussed in Section 5, with particular respect to time-varying loan to value ratios, there may in some instances be an argument for using legal prohibitions to help police the boundary between regulated and unregulated functions.

When a financial crisis does occur, it, usually, first attacks the unprotected sector, as occurred with SIVs and conduits in 2007. But the existence of the differential between the protected and unprotected sector then has the capacity to make the crisis worse. When panic and extreme risk aversion take hold, the depositors in, and creditors to, the unprotected, or weaker, sector seek to withdraw their funds, and place these in the protected, or stronger, sector, thereby redoubling the pressures on the weak and unprotected sectors, who are then forced into fire sales of assets, etc. The combination of a boundary between the protected and the unprotected, with greater constraints on the business of the regulated sector, almost guarantees a cycle of flows into the unregulated part of the system during cyclical expansions with sudden and dislocating reversals during crises.

Exactly the same arguments can be deployed against the proposals that we have made, in Section 3, for time-varying capital requirements.[54] And much the same criticism can also be applied to other proposals, such as the reversion to the use of a leverage ratio for capital adequacy requirements, that might limit credit expansion and leverage in the boom.

What we observe in this latest financial cycle has been, first, a huge expansion of credit, a massive rise in leveraging during the upswing, followed by the crisis, curtailment of credit expansion and major deleveraging with severe, and continuing, effects on the real economy. For reasons which are by now widely understood, the present regulatory system (comprising the Basel requirements and the move to mark-to-market accounting practices) not only did too little to restrain the upswing, but is also exacerbating the downturn. In other words it is highly

---

57 And in op-ed articles in the *Financial Times*, 'A proposal how to avoid the next crash', January 30, 2008, and 'A party pooper's guide to financial stability', June 4, 2008, by Goodhart and Persaud. This in the former paper,

> 'We propose that bank capital requirements should not only be contra-cyclical but also related to the rate of change of bank lending and asset prices in the relevant sectors. The capital adequacy requirement on mortgage lending could be linked to the rise in both mortgage lending and housing prices, and lending to construction and property companies to the rise in such lending and in commercial property prices.'

procyclical.

So the obvious answer would seem to be to switch to a system which restrains credit expansion and excess leverage in the upturn, and relaxes such regulatory requirements when managers are themselves more risk averse and cautious in the downturn. What regulation needs to do is to counter the natural proclivities of managers, (by the appropriate adjustment of incentives, sanctions and trade-offs), not to try to mimic them, (as in the boast that Basel II sets regulatory capital closer to the economic capital desired by bank managers). This is the rationale for having some mechanism, whether time-varying risk-weighted CARs or a leverage ratio, or any other such, that restrains the regulated from such credit expansion in an upswing. It is, at least, arguable that raising capital ratios in asset booms should not really be seen as a 'burden', since it actually corresponds to an underlying increase in latent risk. A really far-sighted manager would do the same, but the pressures of herd mentality, competition for market share, etc., make it just too difficult for most managers to sit out the dance.

Suppose that such counter-cyclical adjustment can be done successfully.[58] Capital requirements are ratcheted up enough in good times to prevent the regulated expanding as much as they otherwise would. The result, as with narrow banks, would be to lessen the profitability and returns on the regulated, relatively to the unregulated at such times. There is sure to be, or to develop, a boundary problem. During good times funds will flow from the regulated to the unregulated, and the regulated will seek to find ways of transferring business to unregulated associates. During crises the flow will reverse, likely with serious adverse consequences. Our own proposals are just as subject to this generic boundary problem as any other. If financial regulation is effective, it will have to face the boundary problem.

Since the problem is caused by boundaries between the more and the less regulated, one extreme solution might be to regulate either no financial institution, or all of them alike. Both proposals have some adherents, with some advocating 'free banking' , constrained by market discipline alone, and others a completely controlled financial system, as for example practiced in most countries until the 1960s. Neither extreme would seem feasible; 'free banking'[59] would, we believe, lead to results that would be politically and socially unacceptable, whereas totally controlled financial intermediation is inconsistent with a free market capitalist economy, especially so if exchange controls on capital flows would be needed to prevent disintermediation abroad. So if the extremes are eliminated, financial regulators and supervisors will always operate in an interior space, in which there is certain to be a 'boundary problem'.

The unregulated, however, often depend on services, e.g. payment and administrative, and on back-up lines of credit from the regulated. Indeed, the unregu-

---

58 The Central Bank that has tried hardest to introduce counter-cyclical measures is the Banco de España, notably with its time-varying requirements for loan loss provisioning, see de Lis, et al (2000). Unfortunately the application of the latest international accounting rules means that this measure may now have to be abandoned, or at least completely recast. Nevertheless, despite having a construction boom far larger proportionality than in the USA or the UK, the banking system in Spain has, so far, been relatively unaffected by the international financial turmoil.

59 Even here a boundary problem of a kind remains. Cash is guaranteed against default; under 'free banking' deposits are not. So in good times people place their money in bank deposits, withdrawing back to cash in crises, thereby exacerbating the crisis. Without this boundary problem, 'free bank-

lated are frequently associates, or off-shoots, to the regulated. So cannot one maintain the boundary without excessive difficulty by some combination of prohibition on the regulated maintaining associated unregulated entities, and of limitations on the regulated's ability to provide credit (even on a contingent basis), (and services?) to the unregulated? We have already noted some of the main arguments against legal prohibition. Moreover, how could one prevent a foreign bank providing such services? Even if one could, and wanted to, draw a strict dividing line between, say, regulated banks and unregulated hedge funds, would it not be possible for hedge funds jointly to establish a separate central institution to provide them with quasi-banking services, including the provision of credit? If the unregulated become, as a result of regulation, more profitable than the regulated, over a long enough run of years for this to become publicly apparent, the unregulated will, one way or another, always be able to attract enough funding for extra expansion, however severely the dividing line between the regulated and the unregulated may be drawn.

Recognition that such a problem is generic may help to mitigate it. Many regulators/supervisors appeared to have been taken largely unawares by banks' reliance on associated SIVs, etc., in 2007. They should not have been. Any new regulation, such as Basel I, Basel II, or time-varying CARs such as here, will bring with it new boundary problems. Any supervisor must try to learn how the regulated are seeking to avoid the constraints placed upon them, (and if the regulated are not doing so, it may be an indication that the regulation is just ineffective!).

Although boundary problems are a generic consequence of effective financial regulation, it does not mean that all such regulation is a waste of time, nor that such problems cannot be mitigated by sensible design. We turn next to some proposals for setting the boundary in a manner that can help to lessen such problems.

So what should regulators/supervisors do in this respect? They should start by trying to list the key financial markets and systems in their own country. Having done so, they should review whether and which financial institutions are so important to the functioning of that market, or system, that their downfall, whether in the form of bankruptcy or major deleveraging, would seriously disrupt the operations of that market or system. Having done so, they could give the financial institutions involved a choice, either to reduce their exposure to this market (or system), or to be regulated. For example, any hedge fund with a total size beyond some limit, or involvement in any market beyond some scale, would be more closely supervised; otherwise more lightly, or possibly not at all. Most would avoid any such supervision. But that would be all to the good. The aim would be to keep funds small and diversified enough so that they can be allowed to fail.[60] This, however, ignores the problem of herd behaviour among small, and medium, sized financial institutions. A way of dealing with this was discussed in Section 3.

In essence the financial supervisors have got to ask themselves, which financial

60 This solution is similar to the one proposed in Hüpkes (2004), 'Protect functions, not institutions'. In addition, that article suggests that some critical functions could be performed by quasi-public utilities (e.g. CLS bank). Note that the US does have a 10% limit on the market share of banks in domestic deposits (subject to some exceptions, plus additional limits for business in individual states). One consequence of a rule that requires an activity to be regulated once a certain size is reached is a clustering of activities just below the ceiling. This suggests that it serves as a boundary. Such rules exist for some trading activities.

institutions can be allowed to fail, and which cannot. Those that they claim cannot be allowed to fail, should be specifically regulated. The criteria for regulation should be made public. Any institution which is regulated as too important to fail, should be allowed to appeal against that ruling, and should also have the option to avoid regulation by downsizing. Besides occasions of institutional downfall, regulators need to be concerned with such market failures as may lead to resource misallocations, e.g. in the guise of asset bubbles and busts.

What difference would this approach make? Probably not much. The few remaining large US investment houses have already come under the Fed's umbrella, but it is equally important that the myriad of small broker/dealers do not get lumbered with unnecessary regulation. Similarly, supervisors need to assess when hedge funds, and other financial institutions, e.g. monoline insurers or private equity funds, become so large and prominent in certain key markets that their failure could completely disrupt the functioning of those markets.[61] A further problem arising from the activities of hedge funds, private equity, prop trading, etc., is the 'crowded trade'. Apart from more required transparency, it is hard to see how this can be avoided.

This could, perhaps, be as market-related regulation. Moreover as markets change and develop, so should the Boundary change. Also note that the Boundary does depend on the estimated effects of failure. Only those institutions so big and connected that their failure would dislocate the key financial markets would be regulated. There is no case for regulating all broker/dealers or hedge funds, only a handful of those that are so large that their failure would disrupt the financial system.

A major problem is that the more effective regulation becomes, the more unpopular it will be, since it will prevent the regulated from doing what they want to do.[62] The Boundary problem will worsen such unpopularity. It leads to the following claims; that such regulation is:-

a) Ineffective and unfair, resulting in disintermediation;
b) Inefficient and cost enhancing;
c) Complex and capable of being subverted.

Let us take each charge in turn. If there is a Boundary problem, (and regulation within the Boundary is effective), then, almost by definition, there can be no level-playing-field. The unregulated outside the Boundary have a stronger competitive position than those within. Not only could this be described as unfair, but business will be bound to flow from the regulated to the unregulated, in other words disintermediation will occur. Moreover, there will be less information about the unregulated, and their risk management may be even worse. So the resulting financial booms and crises could even be enhanced. What the regulators will have

61 Although credit ratings agencies have played an influential role, the failure of one of the big ones would be a nuisance, but would not completely disrupt financial markets. There is no case for their regulation under this criterion.

62 For such reasons Basel II was rather popular with the large international banks. During booms when these banks wanted to expand, Basel II provided no constraint. During the latest financial crisis, when a combination of panic, market forces and self-preservation has been causing banks to cut back on lending and to delever anyhow they can then blame the regulators for their restrictive policies.

done is to take the business away from the regulated (the good guys in white hats) and given it to the unregulated (the bad guys in black hats).

And all that is true up to a point. The point is that the aim of the exercise is to prevent the key financial institutions from overstretching themselves, and so failing, rather than preventing any financial institution from doing the business, if it thinks it profitable. During property boom and bubbles a local national regulator ought to be thankful if lending into such a boom does become diverted elsewhere.[63] An example was when Canary Wharf, the large London city office project, was financed by foreign, not British banks; the British bank regulators felt relief.

An example of the difficulty of the Boundary problem is the British fringe bank crisis in 1973/74. Because of prior constraints (only partially regulatory), much property finance was then done by the 'fringe banks' outside the framework of controls, and financed in the wholesale market. When the British property market collapsed in Autumn 1973, so did the fringe banks. The Bank organised a 'Lifeboat' to save the better elements of the Fringe; having discovered that it was felt in the event necessary to rescue these, the logical next step was to extend the Boundary to cover all banks, as done in the 1979 Banking Act.

So the first problem with effective regulation is that it will induce an unlevel-playing-field, which is unfair, and will cause disintermediation, which will negate some of the purpose of the exercise. And these criticisms are correct up to a point. Ways of dealing with it include trying to arrange regulation so that its effects only bite some of the time, when additional restraint is really needed, so that the costs and benefits to the regulated are not too far out of line,[64] and trying to limit the potential extent of disintermediation.[65]

The next criticism of effective regulation is that it will often be inefficient and lead to higher costs. The financial intermediaries within the boundary are often the most efficient. If their costs are raised, e.g. by higher CARs, then they will have to respond by raising the spread between interest rates on liabilities and on assets. The interest rates charged to borrowers will rise. When regulation is really needed, in asset bubbles, the outlook is generally optimistic. Everything looks good. As Alan Greenspan noted, no one can easily distinguish between an unsustainable asset bubble and a beneficial change in fundamentals. A regulatory initiative that has the effect of artificially raising interest rates, or tightening other borrowing conditions, e.g. LTVs, to borrowers at the height of the boom will be extremely unpopular to borrowers, banks and politicians. Moreover, in so far as the regula-

63 A major problem with the strategy of originate to distribute was that the distribution was often phony, originate and pretend to distribute to associated conduits, SIVs, etc., which were often artificially beyond the boundary, but where the risk and balance sheet burden flowed back to the main bank as soon as the market turned sour. While forcing all banks to retain some residual proportion of securitised products may well be desirable, in order to encourage properly diligent monitoring, the banks that got into worst trouble with CDOs and RMBS were those that retained, or were forced to take back onto their books, too much of such products.

64 For example the provision of deposit insurance to bank depositors should allow banks to obtain retail funding more cheaply.

65 A key component of time-varying regulatory controls could be the imposition of time-varying upper limits on loan to value ratios for residential mortgages. Such limits can be easily avoided by having a market for second mortgages, or by booking such mortgages abroad. But this could be deterred by making residential mortgage debts only legally recoverable if financed by a first mortgage issued by a bank sited in the country, i.e. including subsidiaries but not branches of foreign banks.

tion succeeds in averting a future bust, it may then also have appeared to have been unnecessary!

It takes a lot of courage to take away the punch-bowl just as the party gets going. Even if regulators had sufficient instruments, (which they do not now have), to restrain cycles in credit expansion and asset prices, would they have the courage to use them, in the face of uncertainty in need and probable vilification in practice? One partial answer to such a 'time inconsistency' problem is to put more reliance on procedural rules, i.e. to state publicly in advance that regulation will be tightened in certain specified conditions, (e.g. when housing prices, according to index X, rise at an annual rate faster than Y; when overall bank credit in the country grows faster than Z; when lending by bank I grows faster than annual rate J, etc., etc.). Preferably there should be a ladder of responses, not a single trigger point. The FDIC Improvement Act of 1991 in the USA is an example of a proper regulatory procedure.

The more effective regulation is, the greater the incentive to find ways around it. With time and considerable money at stake, those within the regulatory boundary will find ways around any new regulation. The obvious danger is that the resultant dialectic between the regulator and the regulated will lead to increasing complexity, as the regulated find loop-holes which the regulators then move (slowly) to close. Basel I metamorphosis into Basel II. So the process becomes ever more complex, almost certainly without becoming less porous.

How can one halt the onward march of this dialectic? This is not an easy task. One approach, as already noted, is to limit the periods in which regulation is effectively biting to those few in which it is essential, so that the overall costs, and hence the incentive to avoid, such regulation is lessened. Another, and perhaps more important, solution is to place the boundary at a point where flows across the boundary, substitution between claims on intermediaries within, and without, the boundary are likely to be relatively low. As described earlier, it is such flows that cause the main problems.

A key issue here relates to hedge funds. The aim should be to leave such funds outside the regulatory net, unless they become so large (or so connected with a key market) that their failure would be systemically catastrophic. But if ordinary people should begin to switch en masse between hedge funds and bank deposits, that would no longer be feasible. The authorities should require that all hedge funds operating in their own country impose high minimum limits on inward investment, or have available lock-up conditions on invested funds (so that outflows during crises can be constrained). It is bad enough that pension funds are already investing in hedge funds. The need is to insure that hedge funds will continue to be allowed to fail without public support.[66]

Moreover, should larger banks be more toughly regulated than smaller banks, or non-bank intermediaries, such as money market funds, this too would lead to boundary problems, with outwards flows to the less regulated in good times offset by a reverse rush during panics.

The other main issue is the incentive for intermediaries caught within the regulatory boundary to establish associated entities outside, to which business can be

66 Maybe the need is not so much to regulate hedge funds, but to limit the extent to which pension funds and life insurance companies can invest in them.

transferred. This is an obvious response for the regulated. So it was surprising, at least in retrospect, that regulators/supervisors appeared to have been often less than fully apprised, in 2006/7, of the development, and implications, of the chain of associate entities that banks had set up for this purpose. Some of these entities were legally separate, but remained reputationally connected. In that case how far will, or can, the bank within the regulatory system allow its, legally separate, associate outside to fail? If the answer should be that it may not feel able to do so, then the risks have not really been transferred off the balance sheet.

These problems of setting, and policing, the regulatory boundary are real and severe. There are no easy answers. But perhaps the first step towards resolving such problems effectively is to be aware of them. A guiding principle would be to design the interface between the regulated and the unregulated in such a way that the resulting incentive to shift business into unregulated channels, because of regulation, was so low that it never became systemic. Perhaps one conclusion from this is that regulation should be designed only to bite occasionally. If so, the time when it should bite is, surely, during periods of optimism, risk-seeking and rapid credit expansion, rather than at present when regulation tends to bite hardest just when the regulated are in any case most risk averse.

Discussion and Roundtables

Session 1: Presentation of the Geneva Report (Chapters 1-3)

***Gertrude Tumpel-Gugerell**, Member of the Executive Board, European Central Bank, Frankfurt.*
In opening the session, **Gertrude Tumpel-Gugerell** outlined two crucial questions, relating to the boundaries of regulation, as dealt with in the annex of the Report, and to how to determine the right level of credit.

***Mark Carey**, Advisor, International Finance, Federal Reserve Board, Washington DC.*
Mark Carey welcomed the Report, but noted that he departed from the authors a little in the broad sweep of the text. In his view, the Report, in its emphasis, did not pay enough attention to several of the key features of the current crisis, and in particular, that if the suggestion by the authors to essentially enrich capital regulation was followed, we would not be helping ourselves in the future.

He focused on two main take-aways:

(i) That a better balance is needed between the focus of the last 20 years in financial regulation which has centred on containing moral hazard and the focus of the previous decades, at least in the United States, which has been on bank runs as the key problem. In pre-1980s banking crises, the intellectual tradition, the rationale for prudential regulation and supervision was very much one centred on the existence of bank runs. These lead to fire sales, which alongside the contractions in lending generated, have large negative externalities. In the current crisis, although the press don't make this clear, bank runs are again at the centre of the story. Central bankers do not talk about this much because of the fear of worsening the crisis of confidence. But essentially, every bank that has fallen recently, either in absolute failure or acquired at a fire-sale price, has done so precisely because they were experiencing a killer run.

(ii) A concern that our understanding of what capital regulation does in the current environment might be fundamentally flawed, in particular, that capital regulation may make things worse in a world of runs, not because of the usual pro-cyclical arguments and the problem of calibration, but because the very existence of formal capital minimums may actually increase the likelihood and the rate of runs in a systemic episode.

Carey outlined a few additional points. With reference to the third chapter, he noted that the official sector needed to make considerable progress on the issue of who is going to be regulated and how. The umbrella of regulation would have to be expanded relative to its pre-crisis state because of interconnectedness. But, he argued, no one has really thought in great detail about why this should be the case. He welcomed the Report in making a start on these issues.

On the issue of macro prudential regulation and supervision, he agreed that this was something that would need to be invested in, but noted that, at the Federal Reserve, there was no one who knew how to do this. As a result, the Fed would be rather concerned if it thought the world was relying on its ability to do this well in the next few years. Investment would be needed to learn how to do this well, but if stability was going to be entirely dependent on the ability of a central bank to do this well, this would most certainly be a source of concern.

Another key point about the current run, noted Carey, was that lender of last resort facilities, which were very much the focus of stability maintenance before 1980, at least in the United States, have been ineffective. This was the key policy failure. Lender of last resort facilities are the foundation of systemic defence – this is implicit in the Report, when the authors note that liquidity is not a pool that is sitting there ready to be drawn upon but rather something that disappears into the private sector sphere in a systemic crisis. Only governments can replace this withdrawn liquidity and the tool for doing this, the discount window in the United States, turned out to be completely ineffective in the initial stages of the crisis. Indeed, the Fed has had to learn how to use this again, in ways that have been rather uncomfortable. If there is a strong lender of last resort, one that works in a crisis, macro prudential regulation and supervision will be less essential because the fire-sale cycle will be dampened by the availability of liquidity to solvent, but illiquid institutions in a systemic event. This could perhaps make moral hazard worse, but he stressed, there is going to have to be a trade-off between containing runs effectively and containing moral hazard. It is certainly an uncomfortable trade-off but one that is unavoidable. It is a trade-off that has not been made well or that policymakers have not really been conscious of in the last 20 years.

On the question of capital regulation, Carey noted that the minimum, which had turned out to amount to the well-capitalized threshold in the prompt corrective action tool of the US, is treated by the markets as a run trigger. Indeed, if one was watching Bloomberg every hour over the last year, the following would play out: a rumour would surface that the 'Bank X' needed to raise capital because it would soon have to write off yet more assets. The next day, there would be a rumour that 'Bank X' was going to have to write off yet more assets. One day later, there would be another rumour that 'Bank X' was going to be unable to raise capital. At this point, 'Bank X' has three choices: (i) it can somehow, in some way, raise capital, which, if this worked, and even if the amount was small, would enable the bank to survive; (ii) 'Bank X' can fail to raise capital, in which case a run would commence and the bank would fail within the week or two; and (iii) if the failure of 'Bank X' to raise capital resulted in a widespread run, the authorities would intervene.

This threshold, although not formally applied in Europe, was exported by the US to Europe, in part by the rating agencies. Because these compare international banks to each other, European banks had to similarly remain above the well-capitalized threshold of 10% as was the case with US banks. In such a situation, the weak sheep in the herd, the bank that would fall below the 10% threshold, would effectively fail. The situation was not helped by the fact that official sector rhetoric in the crisis continued to focus on the need to contain moral hazard. This only served to convince debt holders, the uninsured liability holders of banks, that they could expect to bear losses in the event of a problem, in the event of a seizure by the government of the bank in distress.

With respect to the lender of last resort facility, the main lesson learnt from the Northern Rock episode was that to turn to the discount window would mean failure. This is when the retail run effectively started. Going forward, what this means is that unless it is possible to completely conceal the use of the lender of last resort facility, which is most likely not possible, policymakers must be gutsy – when a bank is experiencing a run, even if the policymaker does not know for sure whether the bank is solvent, and even if they think it is, he must sustain the institution for a long time until the market decides that it is willing to put money back into the bank. Should he fail to do so, the lender of last resort facility cannot work to contain a systemic event.

Chapter 2, Carey noted, reflects the literature that grew out of the LTCM episode in the US and it is rather focused on how things work at US-style investment banks. Although appropriate for these institutions, the main problem in the current crisis was not the margin spiral so much as the fact that banks were shedding assets, often at fire-sale prices, and that they were hoarding liquidity out of fear of a run. Liquidity was necessary to stop the run and assets were being shed to either window dress the balance sheet and enable the bank to claim that they had no asset-backed securities, or because they were trying to stay above the run threshold.

The way that runs work is that once enough people are withdrawing liabilities from a bank, everyone must run. It is only rational if, for example, you are a depositor at Northern Rock and you read on Saturday morning that £2 billion was withdrawn on Friday, to run yourself. The key to this, argued Carey, is to focus on the behaviour of the early runners, and it is only the lender of last resort that can fix this. Early runners, the set of people who are particularly conservative, for example wholesale liability holders, or those with a fiduciary duty, are people who want to get out early. They are looking at the likelihood, above all, of official action against a given bank, essentially because only the official sector can lose a bank, notably in a world in which the lender of last resort works. The early runners are looking at solvency measures, perhaps at liquidity measures but they have a distribution of values. When things begin to get a little difficult at the bank, only a few are running. As the bank looks weaker and weaker, more and more will run, signalling to those who may not be paying particularly close attention that it is time for everyone to run. In such a scenario, without knowing the threshold for authority action, which was the case before formal capital regulation was put in place in 1985, there is uncertainty about when to run – in essence this was a good thing because there was no coordination of runners. In the current context, prompt corrective action thresholds acted as the coordination point. Falling below the threshold was a signal for the early runners, the small set of early runners, to run, thus triggering a generalised run. Prompt corrective action has essentially been a failure in the US.

The big lesson is that higher capital alone will not help. Nor will counter-cyclical buffers. The minimum capital ratio in the US is 8%; the well-capitalized threshold is 10%, designed as such in part as a buffer that can be drawn down by a bank in bad times without suffering any material penalty by the regulator. This was known as the well-capitalized buffer over the adequately capitalized buffer. Breaching the buffer should not create a problem. However, noted Carey, market participants reacted differently. To call this a counter-cyclical buffer would not change this behaviour. It might do some good by increasing the tax in good times and thus restraining the boom, but it would involve pervasive regulation and this is something the authors do not seem to want.

***Richard Herring**, Jacob Safra Professor of International Banking, Professor of Finance, The Wharton School, University of Pennsylvania, Philadelphia*

Richard Herring welcomed the Report. He noted that there is never a perfect time for reform. When profits appear to be high and a boom is in progress, few are interested in reform; when a crash has occurred, risk aversion rises to such an extent that there is really no need to curb risk-taking. In this current crisis, he noted however, the enthusiasm for reform is widespread. In general, he noted, reform tends to be incremental, but in the current crisis, it may just be possible that a watershed moment has been reached at which reform will be truly revolutionary, when people are willing to look in an entirely new way at reform. Nonetheless, he cautioned, there is little agreement on what needs to be reformed, how or why. He welcomed the Report as a good contribution in this regard.

The pattern of the current crisis is all too familiar, noted Herring. It began with an extended period of benign financial conditions – the 'Great Moderation' – characterised by massive capital inflows, increase in leverage, a fall in risk aversion as institutions reached for yield, and an expansion of asset bubbles. What was distinctive about this crisis, he noted, was the proximate cause -namely a default on subprime mortgages, a relatively small component of the US fixed income market – as well as the rapid global reach of the crisis.

Herring noted that the authors make a considerable contribution by adding to the usual systemic story. This is usually told in terms of the banking system, because in most countries the banking system remains the most important part of the financial system. It usually begins in good times, when there are incentives to expand insolvency exposure – this is not necessarily a conscious decision but is simply a reflection of feeling 'safe' in a context of benign financial markets. Ultimately, however, the bank assumes greater exposure. Inevitably, there is a shock. Because banks at this point are so highly leveraged, the shock need not be large to raise doubts about a banks' solvency. And because of the particular liabilities structure of banks – a very large proportion of claims that are due on demand at face value – banks face runs. The domino effect that the authors outline is to some extent an old one. The problem is that runs are not limited to the banks that have direct exposure, but, with the knowledge that exposures can be very large, runs occur on banks that are considered to be similar. This causes liquidity induced failures and a contraction of the reserve base.

Virtually every country has put in place a series of circuit breakers intended to short circuit the process before it extends to a full run. Several different components can be part of this safety net. Chartering authority can be all that is needed if this is used in a tough manner so that there are few banks with lots of human and financial capital behind them. But this results in a banking system that is not very competitive. Most countries have given up this model and prudential supervision is what they have come to rely on. This includes both setting the rules and supervision. It could be used in such a way as to prevent all bank runs by constraining the kinds of assets banks hold, but this is typically not done. The termination authority is also a way to prevent bank runs. If it is actually deployed reliably, with certainty, so that depositors are always sure that a bank will be transferred to other hands before it becomes insolvent, depositors need have no fear of loss and need not run. This is the idea behind prompt corrective action. Deposit insurance then acts as a back up in those instances in which prudential supervision has failed, and finally the lender of last resort, at least in Bagehot's regime, lends to solvent banks, thus sending out a positive signal. The fact that this has become a negative signal is the result of the fact that, time and again, the lender of last resort facility has been used to slow down the deterioration of a clearly insolvent bank. Finally, then, there is monetary policy, which, as was learnt at great cost in the Great Depression, must keep the reserve base from shrinking.

There have been several efforts to harmonise financial regulation and supervision, and this has resulted largely in a great emphasis on capital adequacy standards. The reason for this is simple: it was really the only tool that the members of the original Basel committee had in common. Unfortunately, the similarities were rather more apparent than real. No two countries define the capital system in the same way, and most of the time spent negotiating the original Basel agreement was spent defining capital. Attempts to make the standard more risk sensitive have since culminated in Basel II.

Other changes in the banking system that the authors comment on include the increased sensitivity of balance sheets to market prices, the fact that banks are now holding many more marketable securities, and the attempt to create convergence in accounting standards that have focused on fair value approaches. The upshot of this is that capital regulation is increasingly pro-cyclical with a clear and obvious conflict between micro and macro prudential regulation.

A greater emphasis on risk sensitive capital adequacy standards interacts with greater reliance on marketable assets and fair accounting values. On the way up, assets increase in value, value risk measures decline, CDS spreads decline, and credit ratings improve, thus reducing capital requirements and increasing measured capital. Banks tend to expand, as the authors showed well, to spread the fixed costs of the franchise and regulation. Banks may try to lower funding costs by relying more heavily on short term funding, because it feels safe. Banks may also increase leverage and in fact, according to the statistics presented in the Report, they typically do. Any bank that resists on the grounds that it may be too risky really risks being attacked by the capital markets for not using its capital efficiently. When the boom turns to bust, volatility rises and causes banks to reduce their risk positions. If they are using value at risk type models, asset prices fall because of forced sales and illiquid markets, short-term funding in institutions with impaired assets or assets of uncertain value simply dries up, and institutions tend to deleverage as quickly as possible. Rational behaviour by each institution is subject to the fallacy of composition: if all institutions attempt to deleverage at once, the spillover costs on the rest of the system increase.

One of the key contributions that is modelled in this paper, noted Herring, is to update the systemic risk nightmare to take into account the greater reliance on markets and market values. The nightmare begins in very much the same way: there are incentives to take greater insolvency exposure. However, sooner or later a shock will occur and this results in what is described as a margin haircut spiral and a loss spiral, both of which are reinforcing and tend to reduce liquidity.

We must recognise that we cannot and should not prevent the collapse of all systemically important institutions. Enhanced pillar 2 supervision could overcome the deficiencies in pillar 1 capital charges but supervisors have little leverage over institutions that appear to be profitable and well capitalized in the boom when most of the bad positions are put in place. The authors place much hope on rules versus discretion and prompt corrective action standards and sanctions, but these are triggered by cyclical indicators as well as conventional risk indicators. Herring thus questioned whether the faith in prompt corrective action was actually borne out by its performance in the current crisis. In effect, it is not easy to tell a cycle when one is in it. Ex post, it is perfectly obvious, but it is hard to tell a change in the secular growth rate from a cyclical up-phase, and politically it is difficult for officials to intervene.

The new style of run is best illustrated by the disappearance of the US investment banking system. Essentially investment banks became more like banks and a regulatory change made it possible for them to be much more leveraged.

This is reflected in the huge growth of the repo market – in 1990 secured repo credit constituted 13% of federally insured deposits. In 2007, this was 60% of federally insured deposits. We have learned that although this seems to be a perfectly secure and certain way to borrow, it is not. When things become volatile, repos have counter-party risk attached to them and they can disappear as rapidly as demand deposits.

The extraordinary Bear Stearns bailout led people then to believe that the Fed would save, at the very least, the bigger investment banks, and when the same kinds of pressures began to be applied to Lehman, the expectation that Lehman would fail was never as big as that for Bear Stearns. Indeed, argued Herring, it remains unclear why the bailout logic did not extend to Lehman. In large part, this was a communications challenge. But the decision to let Lehman fail proved to be a turning point, turning what could have been an example of constructive ambiguity into destructive ambiguity as the lack of a predictable policy framework undermined market confidence. Markets reacted sharply to the uncertainty generated, notably the money markets, which no one anticipated and which brought a halt to the commercial paper market, as there was massive flight to quality and huge outflows from institutional money market mutual funds. Countries were led to engage in heroic interventions in the system, which in turn led to rampant moral hazard.

On the issue of prompt corrective action and resolution policy, Herring raised the question of why this has been so ineffectual with regard to the large banks that have required bailouts. Could it be that enforcement has been inadequate? Are the triggers too low? The market seems to want a much higher level of capital than the regulatory minimums. In volatile times, capital requirements should rise as a larger buffer is needed simply because the chance of losses is much greater. It is certainly true that the market is cynical about reported valuations. Rapid repeated mark-downs suggest that even management may not know the true value. Morgan

Stanley, assumed to be one of the best institutions in the area of valuation, tried to sell itself to Wachovia just two weeks before Wachovia itself became insolvent. In the end the regulators were willing to subsidise the sale of Wachovia to Citi, which has since proved to be insolvent. The question is then why have bridge banks been deployed or devised for investment banks – indeed six months occurred between Bear Stearns and Lehman. Reasons could include inadequate supervisory capacity, a reluctance to discipline anyone but common shareholders and finally it may simply have been easier all round to find merger partners.

In closing, Herring quoted George Shultz who remarked that 'If a bank is too big to fail, it is simply too big.' As part of the toolkit going forward, Herring suggested that the authors consider how to deal with this particular problem. At a minimum he argued, supervisors should require that each institution have a bankruptcy plan that is regularly updated, in very much the same way that they have business continuation plans. If an institution is too big, too complex, or too interrelated to fail, it should be required to divest until it can be unwound without creating intolerable spillovers. Essentially, resolution tools to safeguard the system against the failure of any institution need to be developed.

***Edward Kane**, James F. Cleary Professor in Finance, Boston College, Boston*

Edward Kane prefaced his remarks by commenting on the need to talk about what the expectations are for the management of financial crises. He felt that there was a gap in the Report in trying to discuss crisis prevention without trying to benchmark crisis management. He noted that he had been arguing for years that the question of benchmarking needed to be addressed, that there was a need not just for banks and institutions to develop bankruptcy plans but that the authorities needed to develop a benchmark protocol for how crises should be handled. Any deviations from this, which would most certainly occur, would have to then be justified as a matter of accountability. Indeed, he argued, we cannot talk merely about the problem of changing crisis management as a problem of improving the instruments, improving capital requirements for example, but there was a need to consider the incentives of regulators, notably the difficulty of selling the notion that one is in a bubble as opposed to a healthy recovery and continuing growth. There was also a need to deal with the incentives of institutions to arbitrage the safety net, to extract safety net subsidies.

The strengths of the first three chapters of the Report are tremendous, noted Kane. The first is that the Report acknowledges that financial crises are inevitable, implying in turn that every country's financial sector passes through a repetitive three-stage sequence consisting of a pre-crisis bubble, an actual crisis or a post-crisis period of healthy recovery. The real problematic, he noted, lay between the first and third stages – how to convince people that the financial sector has passed beyond a healthy recovery. The second strength is that the focus of the Report is on the dialectics of crises, that crises arise from path-dependent collisions of efforts by regulators and supervisors to control leverage and interest-rate risk-taking with contrary efforts by regulated financial institutions to expand these risks in non-transparent ways and to shift responsibility for them onto national safety nets, effectively creating ex ante subsidies which get priced and put into their stock price. The third point is that we cannot just have micro prudential supervision which focuses on the risks of individual institutions and contracts, but that this must be supplemented by macro prudential supervision that deals with the externalities in the operations of particular institutions and markets.

The Report does take some wrong turns, in Kane's view. The first is that theories of financial regulation and crisis generation gloss over the role of conflicts in supervisory incentives that deepen crises. These conflicts expand the safety net and are generated endogenously by government credit-allocation schemes, by lobbying pressure, and by risk-taking at important institutions.

The Report frames the post-crisis policy problem not as one of establishing better incentives for safety-net management, but as one of reallocating regulatory authority (the 'boundary problem') over the shadow banking system and redesigning control instruments, specifically, the range of risks that the Basel scheme should recognize and weight (ideally) in a countercyclical manner.

Coming out of the crisis, then, the central policy issue is how to assess the regulators and supervisors to measure their performance as safety-net managers and how to make them embrace the five duties that they owe the taxpayer. Kane argued thus for a need to measure the value of subsidies to individual institutions on a micro basis and for the need to then find a way to aggregate these values, taking into account the correlation issues across them. The problem, he argued was not one of redesigning regulatory instruments but rather of redesigning supervisory incentives, which in turn would involve performance measurement and the embrace of the five duties owed to the taxpayer, namely, vision (Kane felt that this was where the greatest failure occurred in the pre-crisis bubble of the current crisis – the authorities did not put themselves in a position to be able to see the safety net implications of the complicated securitizations and mortgage loans that were being made), prompt corrective action, efficient operation, conscientious representation (the notion that of putting the interests of the community ahead of those of the bureau and of personal interests) and accountability for neglecting these duties. Any system that does not provide accountability is not good enough, he stressed.

To fix things properly, authorities have to face and answer one simple question: why and how did securitization become incentive-incompatible across the chain of transactions. Why were the originators that were originating loans insufficiently vetted? By marrying the blind trust of the regulators and investors in reputational bonding of key firms to the gypsy ethics of their employees, outsiders closed their eyes to the volume-based compensation schemes that reinforced the short-cutting and outsourcing of due diligence in synthetic credit transfers.

In many ways, suggested Kane, crises resemble a battlefield. The goal of authorities initially at least is the containment of the damage to the loss of life and limb. Under-resourced medics face hostile fire and have limited tools with which to do the triage needed to contain the damage. All they can do is located the wounded and transfer them to facilities that can appropriately handle them.

Every crisis has two interacting dimensions. The economic dimension turns on the losses and continuing loss exposures that wounded financial institutions and others want to shift to taxpayers. The crisis essentially reflects uncertainty about the size of these losses and about who will actually bear them. The political dimension seeks to reduce these uncertainties, to establish confidence in policymakers and persuade the public that the way the losses are being shifted is efficient and that the beneficiaries are deserving. The crisis then ends when the taxpayer loss absorption has finally been capped and the political blame for the debacle plausibly, if inaccurately, assigned.

Studies of financial crises since 1977 show that the costs of safety net support depends on the sequencing, where the ideal sequence is triage – forensic accounting, relicensing to contain the damage – followed by a restructuring of the industry and finally explicitly financing the loss in the aftermath. The authorities in the US have tried to do the reverse, explained Kane: putting the money in, letting the industry and the markets help restructure, and never really doing the triage. Battlefield diagnosis of the size of the problem of the institutions queuing for treatment is necessary. Providing resources to those that yell the loudest is both costly and ineffective. Essentially, the authorities in the US deserve much blame for mis-framing the insolvency concerns as a market liquidity problem and aggravating the twin uncertainties that drove the crisis. In many ways, suggested Kane, we are seeing the S&L mess again. It is not a run, he argued, because runs occur when the higher interest cannot be paid. Near insolvency is only slightly different from complete insolvency.

Whenever government emergency capital is injected, the government faces three challenges: (i) to control the amount of new debt that wounded institutions load onto the balance sheet of the government; (ii) to control how prudently guaranteed institutions invest the funds they receive; and (iii) to extract the government's support as the restructuring process goes forward. The third challenge is particularly difficult – once the government has stepped in, it is hard to persuade assisted institutions to give the taxpayer a fair deal and let the government fully cash out again, and to convince the public that government support will not be renewed at the first sign of another panic. Safety nets instead tend to expand with each new crisis.

So why did the Fed and the Treasury begin so badly in the current crisis? In 2008, argued Kane, emergency capital and liquidity support was not accompanied by a careful battlefield diagnosis of the size of the problem or a prioritized queue for conclusive treatment. An important part of the problem, he suggested, lies in the pressures exerted by lobbying group as well as the timing in the electoral cycle.

As such, the US needs to reform the incentive structure of supervisors, rather than the structure of regulation. In principle, supervisors should bond themselves to disclose enough information about their decision making to allow outsiders to hold them accountable for neglecting or abusing their responsibilities. In practice, institutional arrangements do not hold credit rating agencies and other supervisors strongly accountable for minimizing the costs and adverse re-distributional effects they engender in resolving incentive conflicts.

Numerous complementary actions could strengthen the odds of intervening in better ways in the future, Kane argued. Firstly to improve public service contracting, incentives could be reshaped to confront regulation-induced innovation to offset pressures from the industry, for example through deferred compensation or by requiring agencies to report fully on non-public interactions with Congress. Secondly, liabilities could be extended for bank stockholders and for creditors. Thirdly, monitoring and loss-control responsibilities for competent private parties could be increased, including through public-private insurance partnerships, through the expansion and haircut of unsecured subordinated debt, and finally by devising credit default swaps written on bailout expenditures.

In the longer run, government reforms are needed. Contracts with government supervisors would need to be reworked and their informational responsibilities adjusted. For the market to track safety net subsidies, these must be estimated both by beneficiary institutions and by politically accountable supervisory officials, not merely by the Fed. Crisis preparedness must be improved, through the establishment, publication and regular tests of benchmark market-mimicking plans for crisis management. Government regulation should not be made to rely on credit rating agency ratings, as this tempts these credit rating agencies into complicated securitizations. Finally, the idea of deferred compensation is to be introduced as a way to force top SEC and bank regulators to take responsibility for supervising the safety-net implications of off-balance sheet activities by financial firms.

Private sector reforms are also needed. Three such reforms may be envisaged. One is to incorporate effectual contractual claw-backs for default into the contracts of employees and firms at all stages of securitization. A second would be to require credit rating agencies to disclose the information they rely on and to bond themselves against negligent construction of models and data samples as well as to report not just the rating of an instrument but its downward volatility as well. Finally, securitizers should be required to report monthly balance sheets as well as income statements for the underlying asset pools.

***Robert Reoch**, Director, New College Capital Ltd, London.*
The main elements of **Robert Reoch**'s intervention touched on subprime and CDOs, mainly for clarification purposes, credit growth and leverage, leverage and amplifiers, systemically risky structures, securitization and the strength of the public guarantee.

The business model of more traditional banks, with a basic balance sheet reflecting deposits and lending to homeowners and large corporations was effective for many years, complemented by a very well established securitization market which did just two things: take pools of mortgages on the one hand and corporate credit risk on the other, and sell the risk and the funding of these on to non-bank investors. Until about five years ago, these two industries were relatively transparent, well understood and simple. The mistake has occurred when, for varying reasons, both the demand of investors and the greed of bankers to provide the kinds of returns requested in an environment in which returns were relatively scarce, CDOs were modified to include tranches from other securitizations and other CDOs, so-called CDO^2s. In this way, subprime risk which many years ago would have resided on the balance sheets of banks were securitized in such a way as to become lost in the mire of the CDO market. Reoch noted that only one quarter of CDOs outstanding at the end of the 2007 in fact contained any mortgage risk at all. The other three quarters were purely corporate, but in the absence of clarity, and given the speed of investment decisions, all CDOs were deemed to be risky. The inability then to value CDOs led to some irrational valuations which led to forced selling by both levered and unlevered institutions. All CDOs were assumed to be tainted with subprime and the unwinding of some corporate CDOs led to a widening of the corporate spread. Thus, an initial prudent selling of risks led to both a run on the banks and then a run on corporate credit risk. This contributed to what the authors refer to as the domino of financial contagion. It was unfortunate, noted Reoch, that the term CDO was used for many structured investments; not renaming the acronym CDO was one of the main contributors to the initial crisis.

Why did this not happen elsewhere? Why is the crisis purely a US and European problem? First, complex credit products were not extensively sold by regional investors in Asia, the Middle East or South Africa. Second, products tended to be more linked to corporate credit than mortgages. Thirdly was the widespread use of accrual accounting. Fourth, the limited use of off-balance sheet structures or short-term financing; and finally, the decision making process in emerging markets tended to be more onerous, with more layers, controls, hampering decisions that could not be taken for bureaucratic reasons.

Data suggests that the shadow banking sector was larger than American commercial banks. If one were to include the 30 structured finance banks, which would bring in the European banks, data shows that the balance sheets of these effectively grew from 10 trillion USD in 2000 to 30 trillion USD by the first quarter of 2008. While other products, such as mortgages, corporate bonds, and SIVs were large, certainly in trillions of USD, these were not actually all that big when compared to the thirty banks dominant in this area, suggesting that a large amount of European banks balance sheets included products intended for the shadow banking sector. In essence, there were different leverage stories in Europe and the US. In addition to leverage, in all its different forms, bank liquidity and product leverage, there were also amplifiers in the shape of derivatives, fair value accounting and counter-party risk. The hedge funds are quick to point out that they were not excessively leveraged, but, Reoch noted, the leverage of these cannot be compared because the risk of these institutions is fundamentally different from that of banks.

On leverage and amplifiers, Reoch noted that it was a belief and modelled proof that taking a levered view and thus a risky position on high grade corporate debt provided a better return than an unlevered position on high yield corporate debt. The providers of leverage were of course leveraged themselves, so the first reaction to pressure on their own leverage was to reduce the leverage available to others – this process tended to be done rather quickly and crudely.

Bank counter-party risk was also amplified by risk-weightings. Following Basel I, after 1998, it became very fashionable for banks to buy each others' debt, due to the 20% risk quoting. Particularly in Europe, new bank debt issuance would very quickly be sold to other banks, leading to a situation in which, in addition to exposure through the interbank market, banks had large bank debt holdings. When the fear of who owned what CDOs and MBS came to light, counter-party risk was reduced largely out of fear of who exactly might be risky. The existing bank bonds positions could not be sold quickly, and thus the only quick fix was to shut down the inter-bank market.

Much has been said about pro-cyclicality, noted Reoch. Through the last decade, he noted, the capital ratio remained relatively consistent in the UK, implying that UK banks did not seem to be constrained by the downturn when choosing to lend. However, the effect of BBB/BB crossover needs to be understood. Prior to Basel II, when a company was downgraded to BB, mutual funds around the world were required to sell. Banks, however, continued to hold on, because the capital did not change. Under Basel II, the capital charge doubled when the rating was changed, leading to the motivation to liquidate as a credit is downgraded and just at the time when credit is needed. Basel I was crude but not pro-cyclical. Basel II increases the capital charges during a recession but decreases these during periods of growth.

Reoch talked briefly about SIVs, which first appeared in the late 1980s as a vehicle to hold capital inefficient AAA bonds. The business purpose of these grew beyond this need. But SIVs only faced financing issues when it became apparent that some held CDOs – and yet only some CDOs contained mortgage risk. Thus, the poor explanation of the holdings of SIVs made this sector of the shadow banking sector systemically risky.

Securitization, Reoch concluded, is paradoxical. We cannot live with it – it breaches the line between borrower and lender, forces a reliance on credit rating agencies, allows intermediaries to earn up-front fees but retain no risk, leads banks to become over-reliant on securitization and results in problematic loan restructuring due to ownership – but we cannot live without it, as it removes risk from banks and frees up capital to allow for more lending and asset diversification, creates assets to suit the risk-return needs of non-bank investors, is necessary if bank capital is not sufficient to support the demand for credit, enables risk tranching which allows differing risk-rewards to be matched to a variety of investor needs, allows for the smoothing of income and a reduction of idiosyncratic risk through the pooling of risk, and after 20 years is well established and significant with global capital markets.

Reoch predicted that the banking sector would develop along four distinct lines: (i) banks retreating to the more traditional banking model; (ii) a growth of advisory boutiques, including capital markets advisory, M&A and risk management; (iii) the continuation of the fund management industry; and (iv) trading. On the latter, Reoch expressed some hesitations, questioning where the capital for extensive trading was going to come from in the future.

In closing, Reoch asked how participants to think about how good the public guarantee was. Looking at credit default swaps for Western governments, which have increased dramatically recently to numbers that were essentially inconceivable a year ago, Reoch expressed his surprise at the fact that the risk premia should be so high, notably on sovereign entities which predominantly borrow in domestic currency.

Session 2: General Discussion

Richard Portes *(Professor, London Business School and President, CEPR)* outlined four comments for the authors' consideration. First, he asked the authors to explain what, in their view, was qualitatively different in the current crisis versus the fraught episode in the autumn of 1998, when the deleveraging that occurred was equally significant. Second, with reference to the focus laid by the authors on macro prudential regulation, Portes asked the authors to outline how they would recognise the way the cycle is going, how strong the cycle is, and how far the cycle would go, in a context in which there is a timing problematic faced by various business cycle dating committees (for example, NBER, CEPR) in that it takes time to conclusively establish whether a recession began in quarter X (with quarter X being, on average, about 3 quarters ago). Third, Portes raised a point about the role of rating thresholds. In his view, the role of breaking thresholds should be emphasised somewhat more in the analytical section on marking to market and the role of this in the various spirals. Finally, Portes noted that the focus of the Report was very much on regulating financial institutions, rather than on regulating financial markets. But, he argued, financial markets are just as much in need of reform as the regulatory framework, as noted by Robert Reoch in the case of the CDS market. The issue there is not just one of the central counter-party but includes issues relating to transparency and, openness. CDS spreads have played an important role in all that has gone wrong in the current crisis and yet it is well known at this point that they do not reflect any realistic estimates of the probability of default.

David Longworth *(Deputy Governor, Bank of Canada)* made two comments. In a first remark, he noted that, whenever one introduces a new regime, the behaviour of people changes. This was, however, not adequately reflected upon in the Report. In a second point, Longworth welcomed the analysis in the paper of what happened with respect to leverage, relating to and associated with changes in the margin requirements and changes in the observed value-at-risk. He suggested, however, that it would be useful to think about the capital requirements on the trading book in Basel II, notably the notion of moving these away from short historical sample VARs to long sample VARs or stress VARs completely. Longworth also suggested thinking about whether a minimum should be set for margin requirements, in particular because the leverage of non-regulated institutions depends in part on the margin requirements set by the regulated institutions.

Thomas Jordan *(Member of the Governing Board, Swiss National Bank)* welcomed the Report and the model presented. He raised three questions for Charles Goodhart. The first concerned the introduction of measures. Is there an optimal time to introduce these measures or can they be introduced at any time? Second, if the measures were to be introduced today, would the model imply a reduction of capital requirements even if leverage in the system is high? Third, he noted that the authors assumed, almost by definition, that the model was counter-cyclical through the application of a rule, but is this a certainty? Shouldn't the multiplier in the risk-weighted approach be judgement-based, where one of the main tasks of the Central Bank would be to pass judgement on the additional capital that is required based not just on a rule but on a broad analysis?

Godfried De Vidts *(Director of European Affairs, ICAP)* raised two issues. First, with reference to the comment by Richard Herring on the failure of the repo market, de Vidts suggested that it would not be useful to shoot the messenger. The repo market has worked well, he argued. Second, de Vidts suggested that two new bubbles were arising, both related to liquidity. The first would be the result of governments increased borrowing and unwillingness to pay the price for long-term funding. This would lead to a crisis next year, suggested de Vidts. The second arises from the notion of putting everything in a central counter-party.

Paul Dembinski *(Director, Observatoire de la Finance)* raised questions relating to the notion of externalities which lie at the centre of the Report. What the authors call an externality, he noted would have been called the normal price discovery process just five or six years ago. He also noted that externalities are in some sense a moving target – new externalities will emerge. The question, he suggested was who will be in charge of discovering these new externalities. He also noted that the financial system is a little bit like a Russian doll in terms of externalities – there are sub-markets and parts of the system that also have externalities. In a sense, there are externalities within externalities. This problem is not, he noted, addressed in the Report.

Paul Tucker *(Executive Director – Markets, Bank of England)* welcomed the Report, suggesting that, as noted by Mark Carey, the Report restores interest in runs and liquidity. But the really big question, he felt, was rather a sociological one. It can be imagined, he ventured, that similar points to those being made in the Report would have emerged in the 1980s – indeed, the founding fathers of the Basel Committee would have agreed with much of what is said in the Report. The question is then, what went wrong, and how can we avoid going wrong in the future. Part of what went wrong, he argued, is that we tend to have over-protracted periods of peacetime, and during these periods what we focus on is consumer protection. Indeed, much of the focus of the Basel Committee in the 1990s reflected just that, a drift towards consumer protection. This would explain why, perfectly reasonably, banking supervision was shifted out of the Bank of England. But the question is how to prevent that same drift happening in the future? And how can the academic community contribute to that?

In a second point, Tucker noted that the word, 'rules', is frequently used in the Report. Of course, he noted, in the area of monetary policy, it would be nice to have a monetary policy rule that works, but the conclusion reached already some time ago was rather that what was needed was constrained discretion, as Bernanke would have called it. Tucker queried whether that was what the authors were actually advocating or whether they really believed rules could work. Thirdly, expressing his dislike of the concept of individually systemic institutions, Tucker invited the authors to comment on the notion that if too big to fail.

In a fourth point, Tucker noted that much of the Report is actually about adapting micro rules to macro circumstances. He queried how the authors thought this might be done by policymakers. One of the extraordinary things about the policymaking world, he noted, was that it exists almost in a parallel universe with parallel cultures. In terms of the current crisis, the people who are interested in global imbalances are not interested in the LBO or CDO^2 market, and vice versa. Yet one gets these crises precisely because the particular mechanisms that work in financial markets and the financial system interact with macroeconomic, global conditions. How are we to overcome this situation?

Tucker's final comment was that it is simply too early to know what the remedies might be for the current crisis, largely because we do not know what the social costs of the crisis will be – we do not know how high unemployment will rise across the Western world in particular, and that will have two profound implications. The first is that if unemployment rises considerably, the political backlash and the politically feasible set of responses will be transformed. Secondly, we do not know whether our macroeconomic levers are going to be sufficient to contain the social costs. Thus, he contended, while it was most valuable to hold the conference at this point in time, it may well become necessary to update the findings when we have more answers to the question of costs.

Jean-Pierre Landau *(Deputy Governor, Banque de France)* wondered whether too much was being asked of capital requirements. These serve essentially two functions, he explained: they act as a buffer against losses and expected losses, including hopefully in extreme circumstances; and they act as an incentive to manage risk. For that reason, we try to replicate in our capital requirement regimes the risk management practices and economic capital management of the institution being regulated. Now, in theory, you could do both. Just like in the tax system, one could raise revenue and influence the allocation of resources. In practice, Landau suspected this was impossible. He noted, for instance that, on the pro-cyclicality issue, the more risk insensitive one might be, the more pro-cyclical one would be. If you want a real buffer, you are not risk-sensitive. We also see that in the way we deal with stress tests and tail risk. We all say that we should do more stress and target capital stress tests, but that means having excess capital 95% of the time in the banking system. How does that fit with a sort of risk-sensitive approach? So to deal with that, we all pile up different layers of capital requirements in a system which is increasingly complex. What the Report essentially proposes is to add another layer of complexity to make capital requirements more counter-cyclical. What we really need to do is explore whether the capital requirement has an incentive effect or not, and which incentive effect they do have. It is a much more complicated question than we might think. For instance, if you were to increase the capital charge in a category of asset, you might think that you would be discouraging risk taking but you could also argue that you are encouraging risk-taking in that category of assets to go to the riskiest part to increase the return on assets. So the impact of the movement of capital requirements on risk behaviour is highly ambiguous and not enough studies have been undertaken on that question. Indeed, in our reflections on the regulation of the financial system, we should start from a strong analysis of incentives and structures. It is very difficult to devise the system of the future because we do not know what the social costs will be and also because we do not know what the financial system will be, how this would emerge from the turmoil. And devising the regulatory system for a system of which we are unsure what shape it will take will be difficult. Landau noted that he suspected that capital requirements would in fact turn out to be a much less important issue than compensation, than risk measurement, than valuation.

Sushil Wadhwani *(Director, Wadhwani Asset Management)* welcomed the Report, and noted that his comments were really to ask for more. His first point was to request the authors for more discussion on the potential costs of some of these interventions, of capital requirements and so on. For example, if there were indeed rules to which one has pre-committed, and a technology shock – a positive productivity shock – which necessitates more credit growth than that prescribed by the rule one has pre-committed to, this will clearly have an impact on growth.

Related to that, Wadhwani noted that in the real world, there are living examples of financial sectors which are heavily regulated, such as the Indian banking system, which have been immune from some of the problems rocking the world, but one must not forget the large body of literature documenting the costs of heavy regulation. Some discussion on this issue would be most useful. Wadhwani also suggested that it would have been useful to have some discussion on what would happen if Goodhart's law were to apply to these capital requirements.

In a third point, Wadhwani wondered whether the authors felt that their proposed regime would have helped in the run-up to the current crisis. Some of the information requirements that would be necessary in this regime were just not there ex ante. Finally, in a fourth point, Wadhwani noted that an alternative to the proposed regime could be monetary policy. The argument that is sometimes used against monetary policy is that one might have to raise interest rates significantly and in so doing, create a minor recession. But since we do not know the social costs of the crisis, it may well be that, from a monetary policy perspective, it is justified to create a minor recession in order to stave off a big depression.

José Viñals *(Deputy Governor, Banco de España)* stressed the importance of getting financial regulation just right because this would be an important element in defining the new financial system and the impact that this would then have on the potential growth of the world economy. Three things in particular would need to be got right. The first two have to do with the realm of regulation, which is about having good rules and an appropriate delimiter of application of these rules in terms of the institutions that are covered. The third concerns the element of enforcement, and in turn, of supervision. Certainly if one were to look back, it is not only that there were no rules or bad rules; rather it is clear that the light touch and self regulation may have gone too far in certain cases, but it must be noted, that whenever there were rules, these were not enforced by supervisors. One example of this: according to the new international accounting standards, whenever a new vehicle, a SIV, was created, one was to ask for capital charges. That rule was not applied. The rule existed, it was a sensible rule, but it was not generally applied. It was perhaps applied in some cases, but in others it was not. Thus application of good rules through supervision is key.

Secondly, Viñals noted that at the time when Basel II was being developed , the common theme that emerged in all public notifications and speeches was that the development of adaptations of standards was very much in the direction of what banks were already doing in practice. As supervisors, then , there was clearly not much of an idea of what was going on in banks.

Finally, Viñals extended his full support to the focus given to leverage and increased leverage, notably as an important concept to take into account in regulation. He noted however, that this was also an important concept for monetary policy. He suggested that central banks go even beyond credit and credit growth to look at the total indebtedness of the economy and how this was growing over time. If, he concluded, regulators, supervisors and monetary policymakers were to take account of leverage and indebtedness, this would be a major step forward to preventing some of the events of the past, or at least, mitigating their occurrence.

Ignazio Visco *(Member of the Board and Deputy Director General, Banca d'Italia)* agreed with Jean-Pierre Landau and with José Viñals that the incentives component was particularly important and should be considered more extensively in the Report. Visco expressed doubt that the sole focus on the capital side would make a major difference in moving from merely making incremental changes, as was the case more generally in the past, to a new way to supervise.

He agreed that the macro prudential issue was very important and that it was very relevant to think about how to link macro and micro prudential issues. He agreed that there were significant externalities and that these should be considered, but he noted that there are dimensions on the macro side that should also be considered, such as excessive risk-taking, excessive borrowing. On the specifics of the counter-cyclical changes in capital ratios, he noted that the authors were pushing for rules on the basis that these were necessary also to protect the supervisors and regulators. This might be the case, but Visco expressed some doubts as to the possibility of relying only on rules.

Finally, Visco noted that one issue that had not been discussed was the international dimension. Visco felt that the authors' suggestion to shift regulatory powers towards the host country was counterintuitive, notably in view of the global nature of the current crisis. Visco argued rather that a more cooperative approach, perhaps a more unified supervisory approach might be a better solution than further dividing and segmenting the regulatory framework.

Marten Ross *(Deputy Governor, Member of the Executive Board, Bank of Estonia)* expressed a doubt on the possibility of leaving out interest rate policy from issues relating to financial stability. He argued rather that interest rate policy and macro prudential supervision were two complementary issues. To talk about financial stability without talking about the cost of capital was somewhat strange.

Angel Ubide *(Director of Global Economics, Tudor Investment Corporation)* invited the authors to think about two particular issues further. The first related to the anchoring problem provided by the threshold of capital. One may wish that markets allow you to hold lower capital during a downturn, but you know that this is not true. This has been the experience of the last two years. Markets do not allow banks to become even more under-capitalized during a downturn. There is thus an issue of asymmetry that would need to be dealt with.

The second issue that Ubide felt merited greater analysis related to the kind of financial system that we will end up with. All we know is the system that is currently in place – and this is a system in which banks are mostly asset managers; and asset managers do not deal with loans, they deal rather with assets. And assets are marked to market daily. Thus we may wish that markets move from quarter to quarter, but what we know is that all the banks that have failed in recent years were properly capitalized. The issue then is how to deal with a system where markets are essentially forcing discipline but the information from the regulatory system is that the banks are all ok.

As a corollary, what would be the implications for the lender of last resort of taking a macro prudential standpoint? The authors suggest reinforcing the system so that it is more difficult to break. But the moment it does break, does it follow that the lender of last resort has to forget any moral hazard issue and rescue the system, or not? The reaction should the system break down is one puzzle that would need to be spelt out in greater detail.

John Nugee *(Managing Director, Official Institutions Group, State Street Global Advisor)* felt that the second section of Chapter 2 of the Report was particularly valuable. The problem as he saw it was basically one of multiple equilibriums. If every bank is liquid and solvent, al markets are liquid and solvent, all instruments have full value and there is a solvent equilibrium. If markets are illiquid, banks become illiquid and rapidly insolvent, freezing markets even further, and bringing about an insolvent equilibrium. Most importantly, the system cannot move from the insolvent equilibrium to the solvent equilibrium itself. The theory of multiple equilibrium shows that there is a need for an external operator to shock the system back to the equilibrium that is wanted, and it seems that this must be a role for the authorities, and inevitably the central bank. There is thus a need for a channel for central banks to get the system back to a solvent equilibrium as early as possible, before too much damage is done. This reflects the work done by Willem Buiter, in essence, that central banks are not lenders of last resort, but rather market makers of last resort. They need to come in early to stop the system reaching the insolvent equilibrium.

Alexander Swoboda *(Professor, International Economics, The Graduate Institute)* asked the authors to consider the question of why it is so difficult to get the market to accept a fall in the capital asset ratio in a downturn. Could this be because there is disagreement between the markets and the regulators on the value of the assets or the real value of the capital? How could this problem be dealt with going forward?

Gertrude Tumpel-Gugerell *(Member of the Executive Board, European Central Bank)* noted that there are two different views about the state of the financial sector: one is that we are experiencing a flood which occurs only every 100 years with the implication that there is really no need to invest in better flood protection; the second view argues that the system of regulation needs a fundamental review in its instruments. The Report tends towards the second view. But the main challenge then is a political one: how to convince the group holding the first view to move towards the second position.

She also noted that, if we look back at the history of banking supervision, limiting leverage and maturity mismatches lay very much at the origin of banking supervision 80 years ago. What, then, went wrong?

Lucas Papademos *(Vice-President, European Central Bank)* expressed his agreement with the general orientation of the Report. Nonetheless, he felt that there were several concerns to be expressed, notably on the matter of implementation. Two points in particular. Firstly, what are the implications of Goodhart's law for the general definition of capital requirements and other indicators? Yes, the importance for regulators to look at the true consolidated balance sheet of an institution and to take into account the off-balance sheet commitments is a key element of the lessons that need to be drawn from the crisis. Yes, it is important for regulators to focus on the macro prudential elements, such as credit expansion, leverage and mismatching. But if the focus were to be on credit expansion, in the narrow sense of the word, there are serious risks that banks will try to innovate and bypass this type of indicator. Indeed, noted Papademos, more generally, one can make the point that the more complexity is introduced into the measurement of the capital adequacy ratio, the more complex will be the innovations introduced in an effort to bypass the regulations. The first issue then that must be addressed is how such bypassing attempts can be offset without at the same time changing the incentive structures in the system. Secondly, Papademos expressed some doubts relating to the proposition that regulation be shifted more to the host authorities. For large cross-border institutions, which are important for the functioning of the financial system, such a shift is likely to lead to regulatory arbitrage and may not be enforceable in practice. Such a proposition may, furthermore, not be in line with the fundamental principle of the free movement of capital and financial services. And finally, it is difficult to see how regulation can be properly implemented by the host authorities without having sufficient if not full information on what is happening in the home country of the home component of the cross-border banking group.

SESSION 3: Presentation of the Geneva Report (Chapters 4-7)

***Philipp Hildebrand**, Vice-Chairman of the Governing Board, Swiss National Bank, Bern*

The main policy objectives, **Philipp Hildebrand** reminded the participants, were clear: take systemic risk into account; avoid, at least in the first instance, pro-cyclical rules of behaviour; and, perhaps as an ultimate objective, actually move to counter-cyclical rules of behaviour, something that was being intensively discussed in the context of the Financial Stability Forum (FSF) working group. What we can most certainly say, noted Hildebrand, is that the approach that Switzerland had opted for was entirely in line with the discussion; these two objectives were very much embedded in, indeed are the foundation stone, for what, in Switzerland, the Central Bank had been trying to do.

What are the main obstacles then when we look at the fundamental principles of financial regulation? Ultimately, one of the main problems was how to measure risk. There was no doubt that the Basel approach, whether Basel I or Basel II was very sensible – it is clear that a Treasury bond does not represent the same risk as that of a CDO, let alone a CDO^2. No-one would argue with the basic sense of the Basel approach. The problem was that the devil lies in the details, and the details were inevitably flawed and failed to represent risk properly. The problem then, and here Hildebrand outlined the main differences between the proposals put forward in the Report and the basic choices made by the Swiss National Bank (SNB), was that the very same critique of measurement obviously applied to systemic risk, and arguably, even more so. If it was difficult to measure the risk of an individual institution, it was even more difficult to measure risk at the systemic level.

The multiplier proposed was an attractive proposal. The question was, however, one of confidence: how much confidence could one put in this multiplier, that the ultimate outcome of the multiplication process was going to be an adequate reflection of the risk of at least one, if not both, the underlying variables that were to be used in the multiplication, which themselves are subject to huge uncertainty and flawed measurement. Essentially, what the multiplier might entail was a compounding error problem. If Basel II remains incorrect going forward, which it most likely will, no matter how much we fiddle and improve this in the FSF and elsewhere, it would remain incomplete. And if one multiplies something that is subject to error, the error is itself multiplied. Moreover, as is noted in the Report, and rightly so, the multiplier may well be less than 1. In other words, the multiplier may result in a premium rather than a discount on the ultimate capital that is required.

With this logic in mind, Hildebrand outlined the approach taken by the SNB. The premises are clear, he noted: (i) financial crises will not be eliminated, and (ii) there are fundamental limitations to risk measurement and bank transparency and the ability of the regulator to understand what is going on inside banks. There was thus a need to ensure that sufficiently large buffers are in place. For two reasons really: to reduce the consequences of the crisis when it occurs; and second, to strengthen the banks incentives to behave more prudently by internalising a large part of the downside risk – to prevent the banks from outsourcing all their risk to the government. This is analogous to a deductible in an insurance premium. On the capital side, banks have to meet both the risk-weighted requirements and a leverage ratio restriction. In essence, this complements the Basel risk-weighted approach with a straight and simple leverage ratio – using both instruments improves the assessment of capital adequacy, as both contain complementary information. Using the leverage ratio directly addresses the fundamental problem of excessive leverage. From here, the SNB worked with bands in an attempt to achieve flexibility while reducing pro-cyclicality. In this framework, then, good times and bad times were defined. In bad times, banks had to meet the minimum requirements, while in goods times the numbers involved were substantially higher.

The question, then, was can this be used as a buffer? Hildebrand felt that there were good reasons to think this was the case. Indeed, the higher target rate, the upper end of the band, was essentially nothing more than a rough add-on for systemic risk.

In terms of defining good and bad times, Hildebrand explained that good times are essentially times when banks are profitable while bad times are when banks start to lose money. This approach, unlike the multiplier proposed in the Report, which, albeit very appealing in terms of its parsimony, may be somewhat difficult to operationalize, was rather more simplistic. Indeed, shockingly simple, but nonetheless compelling.

In a final note, Hildebrand expressed his agreement with Jean Pierre Landau that the problematic of financial regulation could not be all about capital. Indeed, Switzerland was in the process of fundamentally reforming its liquidity regulation, a process that was expected to be as important as reforms on the capital side. Hildebrand expressed doubts as to whether these two processes, dealing with the capital side on the one hand and the liquidity side on the other, could be effectively put together. While this might be appealing intellectually and analytically, operationally this might prove to be somewhat difficult. But by no means, he insisted, did this mean that regulation would only focus on the capital side. Liquidity was equally important.

***Stephan Ingves**, Governor, Sveriges Riksbank, Stockholm*

Stephan Ingves commended the Report for its highly informative and well-written content. Starting from the point of view of the macro prudential, Ingves presented the following equations to complement his thoughts:

$$c_t = c + \alpha_L(L_t - L^*) + \alpha_Y(Y_t - Y^*)$$
$$i_t = \pi_t + r_t^* + \beta_\pi(\pi_t - \pi^*) + \beta_y(Y_t - Y^*)$$
$$i_t^{lending} = i_t + m(c_t)$$

The middle equation, he explained, is the regular Taylor function – essentially the rate of interest is a function of the inflation gap and the output gap. In a context in which one is thinking about macro prudential regulation, the first equation can be helpful. This is essentially a similar equation, using a similar technology, but where the starting point is some sort of normalised capital adequacy to which you add a reference which is basically the financial sector loan gap, positive or negative and where the L^* is basically trend growth in the loan portfolio, as well as the output gap.

This kind of gap technology, noted Ingves, is readily available, notably in dealing with macroeconomic issues and monetary policy, notably for an inflation targeting central bank. This was useful, suggested Ingves, as he felt that we should really be thinking in terms of the tools that are already available elsewhere. In order to tie macro prudential to monetary policy, the final element to include is the interest rate, the lending rate in the market, essentially the policy rate plus a margin which is generated in the banking sector in one way or another. If that margin is dependent on the capital adequacy requirement, the issue is clearly then going to be which variable to work on, particularly if you are going to choose to lean against the wind. Should you target *m* or *i*, or both? How do these actually hang together?

How can this be done, then, and is it actually doable? What really matters, actually, is the institutional set-up. On this, Ingves expressed a certain amount of scepticism. It is very hard, he noted, to design supervisory structures such that they are completely removed from aggregate demand management and from the political system. As such, the institutional set-up of any system of financial regulation would need to be thought about particularly carefully.

The second problem Ingves felt it was important to address was, what if market participants simply didn't care about the system that is eventually set up? The third, he noted, was the problematic of the technical machinery that would be required by such a system. Would the analysis be done on a bank by bank basis or would it be done for the system as a whole? What kind of aggregates would need to be used, and how would the cycle actually be defined? Ingves noted that the machinery, in some sense, already exists, and is used in the operation of monetary policy, despite the uncertainties, regardless of whether the models are good or not so good.

On use of the leverage ratio, Ingves agreed that this was probably positive as a sort of binding constraint. On cross-country considerations, he felt that it was too early to say where the crisis was headed, even if the situation looked rather bleak. He felt that there would either be a move towards a pan-European approach or there would be a move back towards a more national, even regional or local approach. The current situation, however, he felt was akin to being in no-man's land, and that was clearly not an acceptable place to be. On mark to funding accounting, Ingves expressed a negative bias, but suggested that a compromise solution would be to tie mark to funding to mark to market in some way, or at least find a system in which the mark to market numbers still have to be reported. On the liquidity charge, he agreed that this could be useful if it could be calibrated. He noted that a liquidity charge is closely tied to mark to funding accounting; in some ways, one is a function of the other, and they are co-dependent. On maturity mismatches, Ingves introduced a different twist to that in the Report. The ultimate maturity mismatch, he noted, is a bad bank. What that actually means is that you own something you cannot sell and you have no idea when you are going to be able to sell in the future. That is why, when cleaning up banking sectors, bad banks are set up to deal with the mismatch issue. On remuneration, Ingves felt that this was a similar problem. It takes about three to five years, he explained, to destroy a bank. If the loan portfolio were to grow by 20% per annum during the three to five year period, a good amount of money would be made. In year six, the bank fails. The problem is essentially the same: a maturity mismatch problem. Certainly, he agreed, there may be ways to think about reforming this process, so that individuals are not paid too early. On credit rating agencies, Ingves saw a whole set of issues that would need to be addressed. One issue, which Ingves felt had been rather neglected, was the rating of sovereigns. It is very difficult, he argued, to set up a proper set of rules to deal with rating agencies, because these are essentially at the same time rating government agencies. On the notion of a clearing house, Ingves noted that in some instances, where markets have grown beyond a certain size so that they become systemically important, it would be up to the central bankers and supervisors to demand that clearing functions be set up. This, he noted, would, however, always be a tough call, but it would need to be made.

On the regulatory structure, Ingves argued that, in some sense, one could argue that the authorities were already dealing with macro prudential issues – in Sweden, he outlined, the law stipulates that the Riksbank is to promote a safe and efficient payments system and act as lender of last resort. In some sense, the Riksbank thus needs to work on macro prudential issues, while leaving micro prudential issues to the FSA. On national versus supranational, Ingves reiterated his belief that the situation in Europe currently was particularly harmful.

Finally on the FSF and the role of the IMF: The key issue in this respect is independence. In a G7 controlled world, an institution can never be as independent as one might like it to be. Indeed, this ties into the issue of naming and shaming. If there are to be standards assessments and there is a decision to name and shame a G7 country, the proper institutional framework to deal with that must be a prerequisite. This is a problem both for the FSF and the IMF. In this context, Ingves stressed the importance of having one institution that maintains crisis resolution capacity. This is truly a public good.

Finally, Ingves closed by remarking on the urgent need for supervisors to go and find the 'lemons' – the banks that are in trouble. As long as no one is convincingly doing that, he noted, all these issues about liquidity, which are actually solvency problems, will remain. Akerlof's article, in Ingves' view, should be read and reread and thought about in terms of a dysfunctional banking sector. It is of utmost importance, he concluded, that the lemons problem be sorted out in the short run, to allow for trust in the balance sheets of banks to be restored.

***Nigel Jenkinson**, Advisor, Governance & Secretaries, Bank of England, London*
As the Co-Chairman of the Basel Committee Working Group on liquidity, **Nigel Jenkinson** focused his remarks on Chapter 5 of the Report and the proposals put forward for strengthening the management and regulation of liquidity risk. The interplay between market liquidity risk and funding liquidity risk has clearly been one of the major drivers of the current crisis, he noted, but the interplay between liquidity and capital, as was well spelt out in the Report, had been an extremely important element as well. The preponderance or the possibility of market liquidity, and in particular, the disappearance of liquidity in the face of confidence and sentiment changes had been an important element and merited greater analysis from a public policy standpoint. Essentially, if people are confident, they will trade, markets will be buoyant; if confidence changes, liquidity disappears. Indeed, he noted, 'Confidence is contagion, and so is lack of confidence'.

On the mark to funding idea, Jenkinson felt this was a good idea, and certainly an interesting idea from a conceptual point of view. The notion of how this would reduce the behavioural mark to market volatility was spot on. Nonetheless, Jenkinson had some reservations in the light of the sorts of questions that mark to funding might introduce, such as valuation. The asymmetric information increase generated would not be negligible. And, given the difficulties that asymmetric information had caused in terms of recent developments in financial markets, particularly in the area of structured finance, this generated some unease about the practicalities of this idea in stressed market conditions. Jenkinson noted that the Report indicated ways in which such asymmetric information might be mitigated – such as having dual balance sheets – and he agreed that this would be a step in the right direction.

On the introduction of a capital charge for liquidity risk, Jenkinson felt that multiplying the modified counter-cyclical capital requirement adjusted for systemic risk in the cycle by some metric of liquidity risk, as the Report proposed, could certainly be done at a pooled level and aggregated. A charge would certainly create an incentive for banks to increase their long-term funding and lower liquidity risk, and that would certainly be a step in the right direction. For Jenkinson, this was an interesting idea, and one worth further analysis, but it did pose some serious issues, as already noted by several previous discussants. In the first instance, was the problem of measurement and calibration. Second, how closely would the metric be to systemic liquidity risk, which is the market failure and externality it was essentially trying to address. Third, was going through capital the right way, as was noted by Jean Pierre Landau in the morning session.

As is well acknowledged in the Report, there are many difficult issues in terms of trying to translate the measure proposed into a practical measure which can be used. In some sense, Jenkinson conceded, this line of argument could be construed as a 'cheap shot' – it is inherently difficult and complex to try to come up with a metric. But of course, he argued, it is not a cheap shot, because one does have to think about the practical application of the measure and how it can actually be translated into something that can be used. Other issues, as highlighted in the Report, include how to think about the maturity of deposits under stress, how to think about the difference between deposits which have been attracted at a high interest rate and deposits which have been there for a long period of time.

Jenkinson had greater concerns about the asset side. The Report suggested that an effective maturity is either the original maturity or perhaps the time to sell assets in stressed environment without a significant haircut. Yet, the Report was explicit on this – the only assets which did not have a significant haircut were high quality government bonds. In addition, he noted, how would one actually calibrate the maturity mismatch multiplier to systemic liquidity risk – this relates to questions of linearity, of slope, and of risk tolerance. How much insurance would one want to have against a crystallisation of systemic liquidity risk?

One key attractive feature of the multiplier as outlined in the paper, noted Jenkinson, was that if you could actually put this in place, a bank with a higher capital requirement, based on the assumption that it posed higher systemic risk, would pay more for a given liquidity risk. Thus, one multiplies up for a given maturity mismatch. The idea was attractive, but was this actually being applied to the system-wide liquidity risk? Jenkinson had some reservations in that respect. Indeed, as outlined in the Report, the situation may be such that no bank has a serious maturity mismatch, but the system as a whole does. Indeed, Jenkinson felt it was rather unclear as to how the measure proposed which was based on individual bank mismatch could pick up a rise in system-wide liquidity risk. Moreover, he noted, how would incentives change if the measure were actually introduced. Would it lead to arbitrage in the direction of the creation of funding chains? Indeed, there may even be questions about arbitrage overseas.

On the question of a capital charge, and whether this might be necessary or sufficient to mitigate liquidity risk, Jenkinson explained that his approach would be to try and find measures that address the systemic liquidity risk externality directly. The requirement to hold a buffer of high or liquid assets such as government bonds could be directly targeted as liquidity risk externalities but there would be some difficult calibration issues involved similar to the ones outlined in the Report. Nonetheless, he felt that it could be useful to have such a stock of liquid assets to improve the confidence of counterparts. That said, he cautioned, liquidity stock itself might well not support confidence largely because this would be a static buffer that could be run down in certain circumstances. A run-down or pressure on such a liquidity buffer would signal the crystallisation of stress and could consequently be used both as a signal and to help buy time for introducing corrective action such as a contingency funding plan or, if the bank is insolvent, the implementation of orderly resolution.

In sum, Jenkinson felt the idea presented in the Report was an interesting one, but there remained considerable value in thinking more about liquidity in the liquidity risk space.

***Rafael Repullo**, Professor of Economics, CEMFI, Madrid*

The key insight of the Report, noted **Rafael Repullo** was that the safety of individual banks is not sufficient for stability and that a macro prudential approach is needed, something that Claudio Borio and others from the BIS have been claiming for years. Repullo agreed with many of the propositions put forward in the Report, but noted that he would focus his remarks on the areas in which he saw scope for disagreement, in particular the counter-cyclical proposals, mark to funding accounting, capital charges for liquidity risk, and finally the institutional structure of regulation.

On counter-cyclical regulation, Repullo argued that the proposals in the Report constituted a mixed bag. On the one hand, there is a proposal to have a low fixed minimum ratio of capital, which he noted was really a leverage ratio, although it was not described as such, and this would be a trigger for prompt corrective action; and on the other hand there is the macro prudential multiplier which is rather linked to the systemic risk story. Finally, he noted the Report mentioned the Spanish-style dynamic provisioning mechanism as a second best option if the first best option could not be implemented.

The first comment was then why base prompt corrective action on a risk insensitive leverage ratio? Why not use the risk sensitive Basel II requirements? Indeed, why have a leverage ratio in the first place? All this, Repullo argued, would need better justification in the Report.

His second comment was to question how the macro prudential multiplier would be set. According to the Report, a 'quantitative impact studies should determine the weight of leverage, maturity mismatch and credit and asset price expansion'. Quantitative impact studies, noted Repullo are based on past data and hence subject to the Lucas Critique. Banks will change their behaviour. And so there is a need to discuss, in particular, the likely impact of capital buffers or excess capital above the minimum required by regulation. But banks do have significant levels of capital above the minimum requirements of regulation; if the regulation is changed, the buffers will be different and this change would need to be taken into account. On the weights of leverage, Repullo noted that the multiplier for the capital requirement was based on leverage, but if the multiplier is based on leverage, the minimum capital requirement is based on leverage, and so the maximal leverage is based on leverage. There was some sort of circularity in this line of logic which Repullo suggested would need to be clarified. Repullo noted, furthermore, that the multiplier is supposed to be based on maturity mismatch, but that maturity mismatch was also proposed for liquidity regulation. In a sense, then, and depending on how one might read the Report, there could be one or two multipliers. One might have reason to worry about two multipliers, for the compounding error reason outlined earlier in the morning session. Finally, the multipliers would be based on credit and asset expansion. These are obvious and used indicators but, he suggested, why rule out other cyclical indicators. In particular, he stressed GDP growth, or rather deviations from trend GDP growth.

On the question of applying the multiplier to systemic institutions, Repullo felt that the authors were divided. He argued that this might not be a good idea, because it would unlevel the playing field within the jurisdiction concerned. For one thing, it is difficult to draw the line; but in addition smaller institutions, with similar balance sheets, may also pose significant systemic risk – what is called 'systemic risk in a herd'. Repullo thus suggested applying the multiplier to all institutions and thus avoid the need to separate one from the other.

On the issue of counter-cyclical regulation, Repullo expressed doubt as to whether a dynamic provision would be enough as a second best. He noted that cyclical volatility of expected losses is much lower than cyclical volatility of Basel II capital requirements. His preference would rather be to stress counter-cyclical requirements with a possible complementary role for dynamic provisions.

Repullo's greatest discrepancies with the Report were in relation to the notion of mark to funding accounting, where he tended to agree with Ingves. The rationale, he noted, was to provide incentives to reduce maturity mismatch and to reduce the pro-cyclicality of marking to market. The specific proposal made in the Report was that assets should be valued and managed in a crisis according to the maturity of the funding of the asset. In a first comment, Repullo questioned whether the authors essentially meant that mark to funding would only apply in a crisis. The main point, however, was that this idea of valuing an asset according to the maturity of the funding was basically inconsistent with any reasonable accounting principle. How would one match assets and liabilities, in a system in which a true accounting principle is one such that all liabilities fund all assets. According to what criteria would assets be split? Repullo suggested that what was being proposed was essentially to transform financial institutions into a collection of SIV and that the mark to funding idea was simply not valid.

On the notion of capital charges for liquidity risk, Repullo agreed with the authors that the reliance on short term funding for long term assets with potentially low market liquidity had been the main source of financial instability. In terms of having an explicit charge for liquidity risk, Repullo noted that the devil was in the details. How would one compute the maturity mismatches?

The simple Swiss approach might not be the best either. Why, he suggested, don't we just penalise short term wholesale financing, possibly net of short term liquid government bond assets. The idea, he noted, was basically to put a price to provide incentives for banks to hold fewer of these short term financing instruments – essentially like using capital charges for operational risk.

Why a multiplier of Basel II requirements, then? Why not an additional additive charge as in the case of operational risk? The approach proposed needs to be justified, he noted.

Finally, on the institutional structure of regulation: the proposal in the paper was to have some sort of modified twin peaks approach where the macro prudential response would be in the realm of the Central Bank and the micro prudential and conduct of business would be in the hands of the Financial Services Authority. The problem, argued Repullo, is that it is not clear how one would separate the micro from the macro prudential. How would one draw the line? There are bound to be conflicts of interest between the micro and macro prudential authorities and there are also concerns of economics of scale and scope. It may be better, he suggested, to have everything under one roof.

The real difference is between the conduct of business and the prudential perspective. After all, the macro prudential can be thought of as simply adding, at the limit, a multiplier. And why would one separate the micro prudential from the Central Bank? After all, the lender of last resort needs to provide information. As outlined in a paper by Willem Buiter, the question of whether the Central Bank should supervise the behaviour of banks has been vigorously debated for years and there are valid arguments on both sides. The Northern Rock debacle clearly showed, however, what could happen when a Central Bank does not know what is happening inside a bank it might be called upon to lend to. It could be preferable then, to go for the conventional twin peaks approach, with both macro and micro prudential supervision under the roof of the Central Bank and the conduct of business under the roof of the FSA.

Session IV: General Discussion

Stephen Cecchetti *(Economic Advisor and Head of the Monetary and Economic Department, Bank for International Settlements)* reminded participants that there is considerable ongoing work in terms of implementation of macro prudential regulations. He shared Ingves' concern about early warning systems in general. If someone is assigned to provide an early warning signal for which there will be actual action, then there will either be no warnings or the warnings will be such that the action supposed to be taken will be impotent. This is serious problem, added Cecchetti for which there is no obvious solution. Another serious issue, he added, was how to deal with the arms race that exists between the financial innovators and the regulators. While there may be something to be said for pushing for the use of existing standard setting bodies to monitor this, as the authors of the Report suggested, there is nonetheless an important governance issue that must be dealt with. The problem, he noted, is that there is a need for a mechanism to manage the escalation of disagreements beyond the existing standards setting committees, to take the issue to a higher level where a decision can actually be made. He concluded that he would be keen to see someone create just such a mechanism, including, notably, organisations such as the Basel committee.

Danièle Nouy *(Secretary General, Commission Bancaire)* had two reactions to the proposal put forward in the Report that more powers be given to the host country and to have subsidiaries instead of branches for systemically important banks. First, she noted, national governments and taxpayers do not provide money for foreign banks, including subsidiaries of foreign banks established in their countries. She gave the following example: supposed there is a subsidiary of Lehman Brothers, well-capitalised, in a strong liquidity situation, with a good quality of management, and where there is cash pooling in another country on contracts of the national customers in the foreign company of Lehman Group. When there is a failure of Lehman, there is not a cent left in the subsidiary, national customers have to pay the money they owe to the French subsidiary to the foreign subsidiary that signed the contracts abroad and one ends up being fortunate if the collateral put in the national payment system helps at all in the end with the national bill. Essentially, there is a subsidiary problem, most definitely in Europe, but most likely elsewhere as well.

Richard Portes *(Professor, London Business School and President, CEPR)* expressed agreement with the comment made by Repullo on the issue of mark to funding, but went further. Doesn't the concern for eliminating duration mismatch verge on eliminating maturity transformation? And is this not what banks are for? If we want to eliminate maturity transformation, then we are talking about a very different financial system. Second, Portes wondered about the notion expressed that supranational supervision cannot work without federal funding. Why could there not be ex ante burden sharing rules? Clearly, the authorities don't want to hear about such proposals, most likely because of issues related to moral hazard, but surely we are beyond that now? Surely we ought to be able to talk about ex ante burden sharing which does not imply a fiscal federal authority? Third, on the issue of exchange trading, Portes agreed that this might eliminate idiosyncratic contracts, but perhaps this was not so important. There are many elaborations in the current financial system that it could well do without, such as CDS contracts of a bizarre nature. Yes, there might be resistance from investment banks that would see their profits fall, but this could be managed. In addition, Portes noted that he did not completely understand the proposal to use differential capital haircuts to shift transactions to organised exchanges. Finally, on credit rating agencies, Portes welcomed the proposal in the Report to remove the regulatory licence, but he expressed concern about trying to adhere to the issuer-pays model, which has only been in operation since 1975. Prior to that, it was the investor who paid, and today, there are actually a few credit rating agencies that do work on the 'investor-pays' principle. These seem to exist and function well. Indeed, he noted, there is a public good issue here, but sometimes public goods do become private goods. In addition, he noted, the Report seems to rely on reputational incentives for the proper behaviour of credit rating agencies, but research has shown that this does not work in theory.

Jean-Pierre Danthine *(Professor, University of Lausanne, Managing Director, Swiss Finance Institute)* raised two points. The first was closely related to the comments made by Portes. Referring to the discussions on externalities and on the notion of information as a public good, Danthine suggested that much of what was going on was the result of information imperfections, asymmetries, sometimes even intended opaqueness. Many of the proposals in the Report were in fact expressing the idea of producing more information. It is not clear, Danthine noted, however, that this was exactly what the authors were looking for.

Related to this was the role of capital requirements and how market reacts to these. Perhaps focusing on the production of indicators and signals of the nature discussed in the Report would be a direction to take that would avoid the problem of market reaction.

In response to the comments made by Hildebrand on the system put in place by Switzerland, Danthine asked how bad times were defined. Bad times meant negative profits for whom? The bank in question, the two big banks, or all banks? Danthine expressed his concern about a situation in which the idiosyncratic risk of the bank gets in the way and leads to alleviation of the capital requirement. An example would be UBS buying ABN Amro and being rewarded with a lower capital requirement.

Philipp Hildebrand *(Vice-Chairman of the Governing Board, Swiss National Bank)* explained that it is the individual bank for whom bad times are defined, and not the two banks combined. How to deal with special circumstances such as those outlined by Danthine would be something that would just have to be managed as they occurred. Essentially, Switzerland is in a particular situation as the macro prudential side of the equation essentially boils down to two banks. Very clearly, this would mean that the supervision of the two banks would essentially move to the Central Bank, because there would be no way to split what is macro prudential and other supervision. As such, Hildebrand asked the authors whether the model proposed in the Report would be applicable to the case of Switzerland.

Hyun Shin *(Professor of Economics, Princeton University)* noted that, leaving aside which institution is supervised by whom, it might be better to say that the institutions and the overall conduct of these institutions would be under the roof of the financial regulators, but the overall regulation, the overall turning on and off of macro liquidity would come under the remit of the Central Bank.

Dirk Schoenmaker *(Professor, Free University of Amsterdam)* posed the question of how to make macro prudential regulation work, what kinds of structures would be needed. While he agreed that there was a case to be made for having macro prudential on one side and micro prudential on the other, and indeed, Central Banks have been macro prudential supervisors for some time now – they all have financial stability in their mission statement – the problem was that this was essentially an emperor without clothes. One may try to make the clothes and give them some instruments but perhaps one should consider putting a micro supervisor in the Central Bank in order to benefit from having all the instruments under one institution. Indeed, macro and micro prudential regulation needed to be very close together – they were both economics driven. You may need an accountant to read a balance sheet but following this, an economist is also needed at the micro prudential level. Schoenmaker felt that macro and micro could be split, as proposed in the Report, but it would be important to ensure that the macro was being appropriately followed up on.

On the issue of accounting, **Paul Tucker** *(Executive Director-Markets, Bank of England)* noted that it would be important to get accountants to engage with the central debate, to get them to shift away from seeing themselves as measuring something rather than acting upon something. The insistence by accountants that they are measuring something is pernicious, he added – it is not only conceptually flawed, but morally wicked given the contribution this has made to the current situation, even if Central Banks as well as the regulators do indeed share in this responsibility.

On the issue of rating agencies, Tucker agreed with the Report's proposal to take ratings out of Basel regulation and noted that the Bank of England had opposed the use of ratings in Basel II. But there was another problem, he noted. Should we allow regulated institutions to be rated? Over the past year, not only in the UK but in several countries, regulators have seemed to be prepared to deal with individual institutions over a number of weeks or months with a contingency plan only to see this smashed out of the field by rating agencies pre-empting them in some way, and accelerating the need for some kind of regulatory or fiscal response.

On macro prudential issues, Tucker noted that one of the discussants touched on the question of macro versus micro regulation, trying to argue that these were in fact rather similar. Tucker disagreed, arguing that, in some deep sense, in terms of what the authors were trying to achieve, macro and micro regulation were not, in fact, similar. Micro regulation was very significantly about consumers, about depositors, while macro regulation was essentially about jobs. What will happen in the Western world, he noted, is that millions of people will lose their livelihoods because of what has been done. If one believes in hysteresis, that is a terrible thing.

On the question of the use of rules, Tucker noted that if rules were not going to work, then one would have to look towards macro tools rather than micro tools, because rules are essentially micro tools. This doesn't necessarily mean monetary policy, he noted, in the sense of interest rates. It could be related to credit creation, and, in this respect, Tucker noted that one of the most important ideas that he felt emerged from the day's discussion was the point made by Ingves on having a policy instrument for credit creation – as was noted earlier, not all credit creation is bad, there may be productivity shifts in the economy where it could be warranted. However, it was unlikely that there would be be rules that could set the optimal path of credit – judgement would be needed.

In terms of the Lucas critique, Tucker noted that this applies to pretty much everything, including monetary policy. What it means is that there is a need to be reasonably transparent about what the reaction function might be. The greater difficulty in this respect would be the fact that 'peacetime' lasts so long and there would probably be even fewer data points to work with in terms of observing the reaction function of the macro prudential authority. It might take years to know what the effect of shifting the basic capital requirement from 4% to 5% would be in an upswing.

Two thoughts in conclusion: on the practical side, it may be much easier to think about macro prudential supervision in terms of Basel I rather than Basel II in the sense that it is possible to formulate coherent propositions about this in terms of Basel I. Basel I basically had a minimum capital requirement which was set for everybody and individual capital requirements set by the micro regulator. On the academic side, over time, we would need Woodford-type work on just what it is that is trying to be achieved in terms of addressing frictions in the financial and real economies.

Claudio Borio *(Head of Research and Policy Analysis, Bank for International Settlements)* welcomed the Report, noting that this was also well received at the BIS, both in terms of the strengthening of the macro prudential orientation and the idea of building as far as possible on Basel 2 in the form of a simple and transparent adjustment. The question he raised was whether the Report actually went far enough in terms of strengthening the macro prudential dimension. There are basically two aspects to the macro prudential dimension: on the one had is the systematic versus idiosyncratic risk at a point in time in the financial system; on the other hand is the counter-cyclical story about how risk moves over time and how the buffers adjust. On the systematic versus idiosyncratic distinction, much of the adjustment talked about explicitly in the Report is based on characteristics of the individual institutions as opposed to characteristics of the system. The common exposure aspects are not taken into account sufficiently. When it comes to liquidity, one is just looking at the liquidity position of the individual institution, but one is not looking at how many institutions have similar liquidity positions across the system. Indeed, the only explicit reference to a system-wide variable is in the COVAR, which is a stressed sort of VAR, but this is not taken further. There is no discussion of how this could be built in to the system, and it would be helpful if the Report were to do that. For example, explained Borio, one could try and calculate the VAR for the system as a whole, and based on that, try to calculate the contribution of the individual institution. When it comes to the counter-cyclical aspects, Borio wondered whether the rules proposed were in fact sufficiently counter-cyclical. It would be helpful, he suggested, if the authors could be a little more explicit about the precise nature of the macro prudential adjustment that they have in mind. For example, if this is related to credit, credit is a lagging variable, credit has been expanding in the current period, and we would have seen capital requirements going up during much of the crisis, which is not what the authors intended. The same applies to liquidity adjustment – this would be highly pro-cyclical.

José Viñals *(Deputy Governor, Banco de España)* explained that because pro-cyclicality is such an important issue, the question to be asked was to what extent would the proposal of the authors in the Report, even if it could be implemented in full, be enough to deal with the excess pro-cyclicality in the banking system? The answer is perhaps not enough because what we may need is a set of measures which can be implemented together. There is thus a need to work on all the incentives involved, to work on the counter-cyclical requirements, perhaps making them simpler, to add the leverage ratio, the old-fashioned leverage ratio which feature sin the Swiss system. Viñals added that it would be convenient to have certain features of the Spanish dynamic type provisions. These had a couple of important advantages: they are simple to implement and calculate; unlike capital charges, they go through the profit and loss account which means that one does not distribute away present profits which are tomorrow's losses. This latter point, Viñals stressed, was critical. And they would change the incentives of banks when granting credit. Finally, another advantage would be that the provisions, by their very nature, are much less likely to be subject to the critique that even counter-cyclical capital charges would run into coordinating problems, as noted earlier in the morning. There is one single problem with dynamic provisions – accountants do not like them. But, argued Viñals, this is a battle worth fighting. Indeed, the Report suggests bringing the macro prudential concerns into the realm of supervisors. In order to have a system that is stable and resilient, these macro prudential concerns also need to be brought into the realm of the accountants and auditors. Otherwise, nothing will be done to deal effectively with pro-cyclicality.

José de Gregorio *(Governor, Central Bank of Chile)* was reminded of discussions on the international financial architecture, on crisis prevention and crisis management. His understanding of the Report was that it was very much about crisis prevention – how to build a solid financial system. But, he noted, we are in a huge crisis at the moment, and as such, he asked the authors whether any of the principles proposed could be used in the ongoing turmoil. On the supervisory role of central banks and the micro-macro regulation issue, he noted that most central banks, in general, have the role of financial stability. In terms of specific firms at the micro level, however, there might well be some conflicts of interest with monetary policy. Thus, he preferred to have this dimension in a separate agency, but with enough flow of information.

David Green *(Advisor of International Affairs, Financial Reporting Council)* noted that, on mark to maturity, he had some difficulties with what had been presented, as it seemed to require allocating assets to maturity, and the potential for putting the most volatile assets into the bucket with the longest maturity would be huge. He also noted that he was struggling a little in trying to understand how the auditors would deal with an identical asset being valued in a different way by every single bank. He thus wondered whether the authors had considered a completely different approach, which had been adopted by insurance supervisory with exactly these kinds of difficulties.

Jacques Depla *(Council of Advisers to the Prime Minister)* took participants bank to Plato's musings some 25 centuries ago, and asked, 'Who guards the guardians?' Who would regulate the regulators, he asked. Delpla felt that this element was missing in the Report. In a sense it was some kind of a Lucas critique problem. Should there then be competition across regulators? Should the implementation of the new roles be left to the regulators, who, by and large, he noted, had failed in the current crisis. Should the regulator be left in place to implement the new regulation? Or should we rely on markets?

Alexander Swoboda *(Professor, International Economics, The Graduate Institute)* noted that, in defence of Tinbergen, it was fair to say that not enough had been said about monetary policy and its role in financial stability. There are times when monetary policy, essentially interest rate policy, has to be aimed differently, depending on the context and situation, and in such cases, it would certainly be very useful to have an additional instrument. In fact, he noted, it is crucial. This additional instrument should, he noted, be assigned according to Mundell in terms of its comparative advantage. If a conflict should arise over objectives, however, the comparative advantage of monetary policy is stability of the price level, and that stability can contribute to stability of the financial system.

Lucas Papademos *(Vice-President, European Central Bank)* noted three points in closing the session. On the issue of international accounting, he agreed with José Viñals on his remarks but suggested that the question was the following: international accounting standards setters emphasise strongly that the primary objective of accounting standards and valuation is really to provide accurate information to market participants. They also say that one cannot argue that pro-cyclicality is caused by accounting standards and valuation methods, but that these methods and the valuation is rather a consequence of the inherent pro-cyclicality of the system. In noting his disagreement with the view put forward by standard setters, Papademos asked, What argument could be made to support the view that financial stability considerations should be taken into account in setting accounting standards, of course in such a way that does not impair the other objective of providing accurate and meaningful information to market participants about valuations. The second point, he noted, is that the crisis had clearly highlighted the important synergies between central banking functions and supervisory functions in managing a crisis and, in particular, the important role of timely, meaningful and relevant information flows between central banking functions and the supervisory functions. In this sense, Papademos welcomed the proposal that macro prudential supervision be allocated to central banks. However, at the same time, he noted that what has to be ensured is that there is a very effective information exchange and cooperation between the supervisory and central banking functions. If the supervisory functions were to be within, although separated from the Central Bank, one might be able to optimize the amount of synergies and information exchange. In other words, the two pillars would need to function within a coordinated framework; they should not function independently. In a final point, Papademos noted that there was one point on which he did not agree with Charles Goodhart, as already noted by Richard Portes. He did not feel that the fiscal powers were the dominant factor for the design of the overall framework for financial stability. While they might have an important role, and clearly they would have a crucial role in the resolution phase, the financial stability framework includes crisis prevention and liquidity management, and while in the crisis resolution phase, there must clearly be consistency in the way that the different authorities – supervisors, central bankers, Treasuries, function, it was to take the point too far to say that a dominant role for Treasury was a necessary and essential factor for the design and functioning of the overall financial stability framework.

References

Abreu, D. and M. K. Brunnermeier, (2003), 'Bubbles and Crashes', *Econometrica*, 71(1), 173-204.

Acharya, V. and M. Richardson, (2009), *Restoring Financial Stability: How to Repair a Failed System*, John Wiley & Sons, Hoboken, New Jersey.

Adrian, T. and M. K. Brunnermeier (2008) 'CoVaR' working paper, Princeton University and Federal Reserve Bank of New York.

Adrian, T. and H. S. Shin (2007) 'Liquidity and Leverage' forthcoming in the *Journal of Financial Intermediation*.

Allen, F. and E. Carletti, (2008), 'Mark-to-Market Accounting and Liquidity Pricing', *Journal of Accounting and Economics*.

Brunnermeier, M. K. (2009) 'Deciphering the Liquidity and Credit Crunch of 2007-2008' *Journal of Economic Perspectives*, Winter 2009, 77-100.

Brunnermeier, M. K. and S. Nagel (2004),'Hedge Funds and the Technology Bubble', *Journal of Finance*, 59(5), 2013-2040.

Brunnermeier, M. K. and L.H. Pedersen, (2009), 'Market Liquidity and Funding Liquidity', *Review of Financial Studies*, 22(6).

Buiter, W., (2007), 'Central Banks and Financial Crises', paper presented at Jackson Hole Conference, organised by the Federal Reserve Bank of Kansas City, August.

Buiter, W., (2009), 'Accounting according to Barclays: declining creditworthiness as a source of profits', on *http://blogs.ft.com/maverecon/*, February 9.

Buiter, W., and A. Sibert, (2007), 'Central banks as market makers of last resort', parts 1 to 4, blog on *www.ft.com/maverecon*, August.

Crockett, A., (2000), 'Marrying the micro- and macro-prudential dimensions of financial stability', Eleventh International Conference of Banking Supervisors, Basel, 20-21 September.

Danielsson, J., Embrechts, P., Goodhart, C., Keating, C, Muennich, F. and H. Shin, (2001), 'An Academic Response to Basel II', LSE Financial Markets Group Special Paper no. 130.

Davis Polk & Wardwell, (2008), 'Emergency Economic Stabilization Act of 2008', see *http://www.dpw.com/1485409/clientmemos/EESA.memo.pdf.*

De Bandt, O. and P. Hartmann, (2000), 'Systemic Risk: A Survey', CEPR Discussion Paper, no. 2634, December.

Ferguson, R. Jr., Hartmann, P., Panetta, F., Portes, R. and D. Laster, (2007), 'International Financial Stability', *Geneva Reports on the World Economy* 9, ICMB (Geneva) and CEPR (London).

de Lis, S.F., Pagés, J.M. and J. Saurina, (2000), 'Credit Growth, Problem Loans and Credit Risk Provisioning in Spain', Banco de Espana Working Paper No. 0018.

Goodhart, C.A.E., (2008), 'The Boundary Problem in Financial Regulation', *National Institute Economic Review*, No. 206, October.

Goodhart, C.A.E., (2009), *The Regulatory Response to the Financial Crisis*, Edward Elgar.

Goodhart, C.A.E., (forthcoming), *The Early History of the Basel Committee on Banking Supervision.*

Goodhart, C.A.E., Sunirand, P. and D.P. Tsomocos, (2004), 'A Model to Analyse Financial Fragility: Applications', *Journal of Financial Stability*, 1, 1-30.

Goodhart, C.A.E., Sunirand, P. and D.P. Tsomocos, (2006a), 'A Model to Analyse Financial Fragility', *Economic Theory*, 27, 107-142.

Goodhart, C.A.E., Sunirand, P. and D.P. Tsomocos, (2006b), 'A Time Series Analysis of Financial Fragility in the UK Banking System', *Annals of Finance*, 2, 1-21.

Hellwig, M., (1995), 'Systemic Aspects of Risk Management in Banking and Finance', Schweizerische Zeitschrift für Volkswirtschaft und Statistik/Swiss *Journal of Economics and Statistics* 131, 723-737; *http://www.sjes.ch/papers/1995-IV-9.pdf*

Huertas, T., (2008), 'The Supervision of Financial Services: What's next?', speech given at 12th Annual BBA Banking Supervision Conference, 28 October.

Hupkes, E., (2004), 'Protect functions, not institutions', *The Financial Regulator*, Vol. 9.

Jiminez, G. and J. Saurina, (2006), 'Credit Cycles, Credit Risk and Prudential Regulation', *International Journal of Central Banking*, 3 (2), (June), 65-98.

Kotlikoff, L., Mehrling, P. and A. Milne, (2008), 'Recapitalising the banks is not enough', *ft.com/economistsforum*, (October 26).

Lanoo, K., (2008), 'Concrete Steps towards More Integrated Financial Oversight: The EU's Policy Response to the Crisis', CEPS Task Force Report, 1 December.

Morris, S. and H. S. Shin (2008) 'Financial Regulation in a System Context' *Brookings Papers on Economic Activity*, forthcoming

Nugée, J. and Persaud, A.D., (2006), 'Redesigning Regulation of Pensions and Other Financial Products', *Oxford Review of Economic Policy*, 22, (1), pp 66-77.

Perotti, E. and J. Suarez, (2002), 'Last Bank Standing: What Do I Gain if You Fail?', *European Economic Review*, Vol. 46, pp 1599-1622.

Perotti, E. and J. Suarez, (2009), 'Liquidity Insurance for Systemic Crises', *Policy Insight* No. 31, CEPR, (February).

Persaud, A., (2000), 'Sending the Herd Off the Cliff Edge: The Disturbing Interaction Between Herding and Market-Sensitive Risk Management Practices', *The Journal of Risk Finance*, Vol. 2, (1), pp 59-65.

Persaud, A., (2008a), 'Reason with the messenger; don't shoot him: value accounting, risk management and financial system resilience', Voxeu.org, 12 October.

Persaud, A., (2008b), 'New twist on market to market stirs debate', Financial Times, November 30.

Persaud, A., (2008c), 'Regulation, valuation and systemic liquidity', *Financial Stability Review*, No. 12.

Repullo, R., Saurina, J. and C. Trucharte (2009), 'Mitigating the Procyclicality of Basel II', in M. Dewatripont et al., eds., *Macroeconomic Stability and Financial Regulation: Key Issues for the G20*, CEPR.

Restoy, F., (2008), 'The Sub-prime Crisis: Some Lessons for Financial Supervisors', Comisión Nacional del Mercado de Valores, Monograph no. 31, July, see *http://www.cnmv.es/publicaciones/MON2008_31_e.pdf.*

Rohner, M. and T. Shepheard-Walwyn, (2000), 'Equity at Risk: an alternative approach to setting regulatory capital standards for internationally active firms', IFCI Risk Institute.

Segoviano, M. and C. Goodhart, (2009), 'Banking Stability Measures', IMF Working Paper 09/04, (Washington: International Monetary Fund).

Shin, H. S. (2009) 'Reflections on Northern Rock: the Bank Run that Heralded the Global Financial Crisis', *Journal of Economic Perspectives,* Winter 2009, 101-15.

US Department of the Treasury, (2008), 'Blueprint for a Modernized Financial Regulatory Structure', *http://www.treas.gov/press/releases/reports/Blueprint.pdf.*